# Flirting
## with the Barman

*Dedication*
To My Parents

# Flirting

## with the Barman

### The big girl's guide to growing old disgracefully

## KATE MULVEY

NEW HOLLAND

# CONTENTS

# 1.

## CRISIS? WHAT CRISIS?

### THE MIDLIFE CRISIS EXPLAINED

If I told you that turning 45 meant nothing, I'd be fibbing. Me, over 40? Surely not. After all, how can you go to go to weekly salsa classes, hang out with 25 year-olds and sparkle your décolleté with an entire pot of multi-coloured glitter, and be classed as middle-aged. Aren't women of a certain age supposed to rejoice in big knickers, wear dirndl skirts, sensible shoes and have a one-way ticket to Spanx city?

I mean, I'm not like that. I still wear denim miniskirts, have honey highlighted hair, totter on icicle thin heels and flirt outrageously with the barman.

There's the rub. I don't think there is a woman out there who thinks that she is that flabby middle-aged woman reading the newspaper with a pair of specs perched on the tip of her nose, and a muffin top hanging perilously over her jeans. Because hitting midlife is something that happens to other people. We will be young forever, right?

Wrong.

Welcome to the world of the midlife crisis.

Unless you are Nicole Kidman, Elizabeth Hurley or Catherine Zeta-Jones, who live lives of glitz, glamour and never-ending sex appeal, this milestone is not only the middle of your life, it is a turning point, a sudden realisation that this is the time when most ordinary women seem to disappear off the planet, never to be considered sexy again.

How do I know this? Well, the other day I was chattering away to a handsome man at a party. He was staring at me glumly. Then his eyes lit up and he did a double take. Had I said something utterly witty, mind-bogglingly intelligent? Had he discovered that I was the love of his life? Then I turned round. A 20-something blonde with bazooka boobs and skin like porcelain tottered past and threw him one of those 'mm, I like the look of you' glances. He muttered, stuttered, nearly tripped over the bar stool and rushed after her like a stag on heat. Tears plopped into my prosecco. That was it. I was officially invisible.

## MOI, MIDDLE-AGED?

Of course, most women are stuck in denial, avoiding mirrors like the plague, hanging out with our mum's friends just so that we can feel like the flippy one in the centre, making everyone laugh. We've been botoxing, sloughing, learning how to Tweet, Facebook, you name it. All this effort because we don't want to face up to the fact that we are nearer the end than the beginning. That we are not that flippy little 'in the loop girl', but more the 'who am I kidding midlifer'. After all, it's difficult to face up to the realisation that one minute:

- You are in a micro mini at a party, the next you are in a comfy kaftan slumped on the sofa with a glass of chardonnay reading *Fifty Shades of Grey*.
- You are parading around in a string bikini, the next you are covered up in a one-piece and a maxi sarong.
- You are walking down the street and men are doing a 180-degree turn as you saunter past in a pair of Manolos and a flippy dress, the next you are filed under 'avoid at all costs'.
- You are jumping out of bed feeling energetic, the next you are getting out of bed because your back aches and your knees creak.
- You are reading a menu, the next you're asking the waiter to hold it for you, because your arms aren't long enough to hold the menu at a distance for the spaghetti carbonara to be in focus.
- You are planning an all-night party, the next you are planning your retirement.
- You are deciding on your honeymoon, the next you are filing for divorce.
- You are choosing inappropriately short dresses, the next you are choosing wallpaper.
- You are avoiding your parents, the next you have turned into them.
- You are dancing to Donna Summer in a sparkly leotard and leggings, the next your children are boogying away to the same song. Everything's a re-run.
- You are buying glittery thongs and push-up bras, the next you prefer comfy knickers made out of spandex.

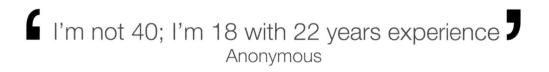

**‘ I'm not 40; I'm 18 with 22 years experience ’**
Anonymous

# THE EARLY WARNING SIGNS

## HELLO MIDDLESCENCE

There was a time when, BF (before 40), it was perfectly acceptable to share a flat with a few friends and live off baked beans and wine. You were allowed to be radical, read poetry and philosophy and listen to Van Morrison whilst sitting on a beanbag, refusing to conform. Living life your way was not just for Frank Sinatra, it was the mark of an individual. And then you grew up, put on an apron and listened to the radio.

Hang on; some of us are still living like that.

Thanks to the baby boomer generation and the have-it-all 1960s, the boundaries have become very blurry. Nowadays, before we reach the crisis point, we spend years skirting around the edges of being middle-aged and it doesn't necessarily mean settling down with 2.5 children and a barbecue in the back garden. You can be 40 and a parent, or single, childless, divorced, reinventing yourself – you name it. We are all delaying middle age as long as we can.

You are stuck in middlescence if:

- You get a tattoo of a flower on your shoulder, or worse, on your left buttock.
- You are a fully-fledged graver (middle-aged raver) and are firmly on the music festival circuit, reluctant to hang up your glow stick.
- When you get to the festival, you make your way to the trance tent and dance all night.
- You think a pair of Converse trainers constitutes sensible shoes.
- You still don't want to wash the dishes straight after having a meal.
- Having a Brazilian is a monthly must.
- You are still sharing a flat with your best friend from college/childhood.
- Your parents are still making your financial decisions.
- You are still watching *Sex and the City* and identifying with the characters.
- You haven't had children.
- You haven't learnt to drive yet.
- You don't have a proper crockery set.
- You still haven't bought a recipe book.
- You are planning on going on an adult gap year.
- You are still trying to get your own way.
- You have an anxiety attack if you are not on the guest list of a party or an opening.

- You feel an uncontrollable desire to dance the Macarena at your best friend's wedding – naked!

Okay, so you have been delaying the moment for as long as you can get away with it. After all, you still look good in a pair of skinny jeans and tight T-shirt – well, good-ish. But then you start to have a creeping realisation that your youthful days are coming to a grinding halt!

And it happens.

> ❛ Middle age is when you're sitting at home on a Saturday night and the telephone rings and you hope it isn't for you. ❜
> Ogden Nash

## IT'S OFFICIAL: YOU ARE MIDDLE-AGED

One morning you wake up somewhere in your early to mid-40s, look in the mirror and instead of a plump-faced Barbie smiling back at you, there is just a wrinkly old trout whose face looks like a cross between Deputy Dog and a relief map of the Andes.

You are not young any more. You have to face facts. You feel tired, your grey hairs are multiplying like rabbits, and a layer of subcutaneous fat has strapped itself to your waist like one of those bum bags you used to wear back in the 1980s when you danced to Bananarama till the early hours.

And it's a terrifying realisation. 'OMG!' you screech, as you take a peek at your derrière in one of those double mirrors they kindly provide in trendy boutiques – is that me or is that porridge in a string bag? You have been avoiding it for so long, but somehow it has snuck up and tapped you sneakily on the back:

So how do you know you are officially middle-aged?

- You have aches and pains – and you've just got out of bed.
- Your wobbly bits have headed further south than a swallow in winter.
- People start to respect your opinions as an elder and even ask your advice.
- You don't recognise anyone your age in the advertisements on TV.
- Ditto songs and films – they are all about youth, right?
- You actually want to live in the country full-time, instead of just at weekends

for all-night raves.
- You wear big T-shirts – not like you did in the 80s, with a political slogan and a pair of Lycra leggings, but because it is the only thing that covers up your tummy.
- You enjoy recycling.
- You start paying the bills on time.
- You keep more food than alcohol in the fridge.
- Six in the morning is the time you get up, not when you fall into bed.
- People stare at you when you dance, and not in a 'hasn't she got good rhythm?' way.
- Instead of wolfing down instant noodles and beer, you snack on pumpkin seeds and coconut water.
- You own a fondue set.
- You say things like 'where did you buy this lovely sofa?'
- You tell people to turn the music down at eight in the evening.
- You start talking about your knees.
- You make straining noises when you get up or sit down.
- The thought of going on a cruise sounds appealing.
- You buy a nasal-hair trimmer.

For most of us, the feeling that the party is over but desperately hoping it isn't, is going to send us into a tailspin, an identity crisis. And guess what? It is happening to more and more savvy, intelligent women than ever before.

## WHAT A FEMALE MIDLIFE CRISIS LOOKS LIKE

Correct me if I'm wrong, but if you picture someone with a midlife crisis, what do you see? A balding man with a paunch, divorce papers in one hand and a 20-something babe in the other?

Think again. That *may* have been the image years ago, but now it is women who are the ones more likely to be tottering down the road in six-inch platform shoes, an ankle tattoo and a 25 year-old rock singer hanging off their arm. You only have to look at Planet Celebrity and the likes of J.Lo, Madonna and Halle Berry, all feisty, fun and over 40, complete with a gorgeous toy boy in tow, to get the picture.

## OUT AND PROUD

The female midlife crisis used to be a secret, silent creature, but now it is out and proud, with a facelift, liposuction and big dollop of hope.

Whether it's dressing like a page three model, stuffing your face with Restylane or travelling around the world on a one-way ticket, women of all shapes and sizes are coping with the arrival of middle age using an alarming set of desperate measures, in an effort to claw back the years and prove to the world that they are still foxy, clever and relevant.

And the thing is, it's not all bad news. As so often in life, things have to get worse before they get better. Sure, you are going to find yourself stuck in a hormonal twilight zone, asking, 'Who am I? Why does my body feel like an alien? Where did I go wrong?' when you wake in a cold sweat at three in the morning. The good news is that this is entirely natural, and if you read through the rest of the book, you will learn how to deal with, embrace and finally come through the other side, liberated and a brand new you.

So, what are the warning signs that you are experiencing the onset of a crisis? You:

- Come home and tell your partner that you are leaving your great career in sales/marketing/you name it, and are off to India to find yourself!
- Suddenly realise that life is short and book a skydiving course in Kathmandu with your best friend from school.
- Start going to three-day music festivals complete with glow stick, tent and a whole stack of mind-altering drugs.
- Start spending as if there is no tomorrow. You come home with a 50-inch plasma TV, complete with surround sound and state-of-the-art DVD player.
- Go into flirting overdrive with the mailman, the pizza boy or anyone else who looks young, fit and free for a few hours.

- Get the words 'free spirit' tattooed on your shoulder and start staying out till the early hours of the morning just to prove you can still do it.
- Start blubbing whenever you hear a song from the 1970s.
- Think you have a terrible disease every time you get a twinge or an ache or pain.
- Seriously consider having an affair with your next-door neighbour.
- Start Facebooking old boyfriends.
- Buy an exercise bike, set of dumbbells and a bums, tums and workout DVD, and exercise maniacally.
- Start lying about your age to everyone, including your mum.
- Seriously consider having a facelift.
- Get so depressed whenever you have a birthday that you go into denial and spend the day climbing mountains, on a retreat, or doing anything that is far away from your friends, family and reality.
- Start comparing yourself to everyone around you and feel as if you are somehow lacking, that you don't measure up.
- Stop buying women's magazines because you can't bear to look at the photos of all those pretty young women.
- Invest in a drawer full of anti-ageing potions and anti-cellulite cream. You name it, you've got it.
- Invest in a whole drawer full of sex toys, from the rampant rabbit to furry handcuffs, fruity lubes, feathers, props and fun.
- Wear big Jackie Onassis sunglasses even in winter – you can't bear to look at those wrinkles any more.
- Wear a cropped, tight T-shirt and think it looks sexy.
- Feel like the fizz has gone out of your life, and you want to get the excitement back.
- Start acting like a hormone-crazed teenager every time you go to a party or dinner where there is even the slightest whiff of testosterone.

The truth is, many things can trigger a midlife crisis. Whether it is a sudden desire to go backpacking around Australia, or the onset of a 'we're all going to die' mortality moment, these thoughts all trigger a lot of strange feelings with the same message: you are at a crossroads and don't know whether you should buy a burka and be done with it, or book a week of intense cardio with the hot trainer at the gym.

You're on the precipice of a midlife crisis when:

- You suddenly look across the room at your potbellied husband and think, 'Who is that person?'
- You find yourself having a full-on tantrum when the mobile doesn't work/ the kitchen is a mess/the husband has left out a pair of dirty socks, or some other everyday aggravation.
- You find yourself having recurring 'hot' dreams about someone and it is not your husband.
- You are terrified you are going to die unfulfilled and alone with just your cat for company.
- You lose your job to the girl who joined the company last year.
- You find out your husband is having an affair with the nanny/secretary.
- Your children leave home and you find yourself sobbing in their bedroom, clutching their favourite childhood toys.
- Someone close to you dies and you can't stop thinking about your own inevitable demise.
- You suddenly realise life is not a dress rehearsal and have a full-on angst attack about how much time you have wasted. Aarrgh!
- You fall asleep upright in your chair – in the afternoon, for God's sake.

Women are forgetting how savvy and sophisticated they are and making spectacles of themselves, all for the sake of a wolf whistle or even a wink from the wispy-haired postman.

**❝** Middle age is the awkward period when Father Time catches up with Mother Nature. **❞**
Harold Coffin

## WHY NOW?

So why now? Why is it that so many women are walking around like overgrown teenagers who refuse to hang up their Jimmy Choos and step dutifully into a beige hinterland of comfy trousers and afternoons spent deadheading roses?

## Fast fact:

A recent survey revealed that 73 per cent of today's 40-55 year-old midlife women are far more likely to say that life is too complicated, compared to 55 percent 15 years ago.

It is simple. Women are different today. This stage of our lives, the middle years, in which women were once over the hill, has changed beyond anyone's wildest dreams. Today's over-40 woman can have a glamorous job, children and still jump up and down in a disco wearing over-the-knee boots and a bra top.

She can fill out her frown lines with gloop, know the inside of a gym better than she does her own kitchen, and can still shop at those tiny boutiques that sell dresses the size of a hankie.

On the down side, now she has to look like Demi Moore, dress like Gwyneth Paltrow and have arms like Madonna. She has to have hot sex, even on Sundays, look as good as Elle Macpherson in leather trousers and make three-course meals in a negligee and red lippy. She has to be a good friend, lover and mother and still have time to bake a cake for her daughter's birthday.

We live in a mad, fast-moving, competitive world – a society that thinks that money, youth, nice handbags and a condo in the city are the Holy Grail of happiness. Self-respect is not about settling down and being a good wife any more, it is about making sure you are still bikini fit at 50.

When our mothers were young, they concentrated on getting a husband and being a good wife and mother. They immediately went from young girl to dowdy, and were expected to wear baggy clothes and have a terminal bad hair day.

Fast-forward to today and we simply don't know what to do any more, or what is expected of us. Do we really have to look hot and honed in a red bikini à la Helen Mirren at the ripe old age of 62, make out that we are having the best sex of our lives, or jump up and down singing Abba songs like Meryl Streep in *Mama Mia*?

In short, we are having an identity crisis.

Here are some of the ways our lives are different to our mothers'.

## THEN

Women:

- Got hitched before their 30th birthday
- Baked cakes, and not just because they had to
- Had a snooze in the afternoon
- Went blackberry picking on a Saturday
- Sent thank you notes after a dinner party
- Played bridge in the evening with the local vicar
- Had a weekly blow-dry and set
- Spoke when they were spoken to
- Put their hair in a bun
- Devoted themselves to their cats
- Wore A-line midi skirts with a pair of sensible shoes
- Put on lippy for when the husband got home from work
- Saved the discount coupons and put them in a jar
- Made jam to give to the needy
- Made their own clothes
- Slept in twin beds
- Saved up for a stair lift.

## NOW

Women:

- Get their first flat at 30
- Go shopping at the same stores as their daughters
- Go to boot camp to get bikini perfect for the summer holidays
- Go abseiling down the Andes
- Use Twitter, Facebook and YouTube
- Colour their hair surf-blonde and try to look like Cameron Diaz
- Wanna party like it's 1988
- Wear six-inch heels – to the school fete
- Own a miniskirt and a pair of designer wedges
- Go to samba classes
- Drink wheatgrass smoothies in the morning
- Wear Converse trainers

- Have a mani-pedi every week
- Blow their wages on a massively expensive designer outfit
- Have a threesome
- Save up for a pair of ludicrously expensive Christian Louboutin platforms

## YOU KNOW YOU ARE A GROWN-UP IF:

One day of course you realise that you can't go on living like this forever, that being cool is not about getting the best seats at the rock concert, but about knowing what the best mortgage or superannuation fund is, or simply putting other people first. It's when having children is something you don't just think about after a few glasses of chardonnay with your other terminally young friends, it is something you did five years ago.

## WHAT TO EXPECT WHEN YOU'RE MIDDLE-AGED

**Failing eyesight:** This is the time when you find yourself with a pair of off-the-shelf specs perched on your nose as you try to read books/train timetables/newspapers – basically anything in print. Whether you had perfect vision or were long- or short-sighted, become middle-aged and we are all in the same boat.

**Talking gibberish:** The outflow of molten gibberish is all part of growing older. One minute we are reciting the words to our favourite pop song, the next we can't remember what on earth we are talking about.

**Being set in your ways:** The problem with getting older is that suddenly the little things matter. Having the right pillow, not being able to travel without your earplugs and tuning the car radio to the same station every morning are all examples. Soon you start refusing dates/parties because you would rather spend the evening at home watching your favourite DVD box set.

**General grumpiness:** You will find yourself getting grumpy at the following: bad parking, noisy public speaker messages, automated checkouts at the supermarket, traffic, the television volume being up too high… the list goes on and it gets worse as you get older.

**14 things every woman needs by the time she is middle-aged:**

- A garden/allotment
- A mortgage
- A proper job
- One holiday a year
- 2.5 children
- A husband
- An herbaceous border
- A dog
- A library full of cookery books that have been used
- A fully-working vacuum cleaner
- A joint bank account
- A will
- A pension plan
- A mortgage

# Quiz

While all women go through some sort of upheaval in their middle years, some of us have just a little midlife wobble, whilst others have a full-on crisis with bells on. Complete our quiz and find out where you are on the Midlifometer.

**1 You get invited to your husband's boss's dinner. Do you:**
a) Feel like running away to Mexico with a dark handsome stranger.
b) Feel frustrated, but scrub up anyway – it's his career after all.
c) Get out your dinner party outfit as you always do – it will be fun.

**2 How spiritual are you?**
a) It's all rubbish. We are going to die, so let's live now.
b) I think there may be a higher power but …
c) I go to church every Sunday; prayer gets me through the week.

**3 How would you characterise your love life?**
a) You are seriously wondering whether you can head into old age with your present partner.
b) You are still looking for a knight in shining armour.
c) You're with a lovable old crank who knows everything about you but loves you anyway.

**4 How would you describe your work life?**
a) You have lately begun to wonder what the heck you're doing in your job or career.
b) You're still driving hard and proving yourself with the best of 'em.
c) You are starting to enjoy supervising the younger folk instead of doing it all yourself.

**5 When you forget a word that was just on the tip of your tongue, you:**
a) Get panicky about having a 'senior moment'.
b) Know that you'll remember it later today or tomorrow.
c) Find it completely normal and nothing to fret about.

**6 If you could really do what you wanted today, you'd:**
a) Get a facelift and liposuction to stop the work of gravity forever.
b) Do something that's sheer pleasure, just for you.
c) Cook a big dinner for the husband.

**7 When it comes to spending time with friends, you:**
a) Wish you had deeper bonds with friends who you could share real feelings and failings with.
b) Are increasing your circle of close friends all the time and spending less time with mere acquaintances.
c) Hang out with anybody who calls.

**8 Do you ever feel anxious about the direction your life has taken?**
a) Frequently.
b) Sometimes.
c) Never.

**9 A typical evening is:**
a) Knocking back jelly shots at an incredibly hip joint for incredibly young people.
b) Staying in with your favourite DVD box set and a glass of wine.
c) Having a dinner party for 10 and cooking everything yourself.

**10 So far my life has gone exactly according to plan.**
a) Disagree.
b) In some things yes, and in others no.
c) Absolutely.

**Mostly A's:** Welcome to a midlife crisis. You are panicking about growing older, you seem a bit dissatisfied in your job and want to run away singing 'Don't fence me in'. Don't worry, read on and learn how to turn your crisis into a benefit.

**Mostly B's:** You are a borderline crisis case. You fear ageing and your life has not gone exactly to plan. Whilst you are having nagging fears and doubts about yourself and your looks, you are managing to look at life in a calm and rational way, for the moment anyway.

**Mostly C's:** Well done! You are managing to navigate the midlife waters with maturity and sangfroid. Make sure that you are not just pushing your feelings aside, however. Putting a relentlessly positive spin on things means you are storing up more problems for later on.

# 2.

# IT WAS ALL A FAIRYTALE REALLY

## MIDLIFE MYTHS

What happens when the fairytale wedding, the dream of writing a bestseller or the life on the crest of the party wave aren't all they're cracked up to be? When life doesn't pan out how we thought it would, women can face some big questions.

Take Sam. She recently had to leave a great job in the media. Now 45, she is tearing her hair out and snacking on coco chips whilst watching daytime soaps in her coffee-stained jimjams. Once bubbly and confident, she shuffles around like Eeyore on Prozac and goes to bed at nine.

Like so many middle-aged women, her job was one of the most important things in her life. Not only did it mean she had a great lifestyle and a wardrobe full of designer clothes, she had glamorous friends and nights out in swanky restaurants.

It made her feel as if she were a high-flyer, someone who mattered. Now she feels about as useful as a fondue set.

Julie, 46, has spent her life making cordon bleu meals for her hubby and ferrying her children to tap dancing classes and soccer matches, but is suddenly faced with an empty house and a husband who would rather be watching the sports channel than cuddling up to her.

These women would hate it if you told them, but essentially their 'happy ever after' myths have been splattered wide open and stomped on by raging wildebeests.

The truth is, women grow up believing in the myth that there is a pot of gold at the end of the rainbow. Whether it is the perfect job and the urban loft in the middle of town, or the myth of the perfect marriage with a kind husband who bakes pavlova every Friday night, for a lot of us, life doesn't quite pan out how we thought it would. We desperately cling to the myth that we will get the bigger house, the better pay cheque or the more romantic husband, then one day the penny drops: Yikes! It's all been a dream.

## DISPELLING THE MYTHS

**THE HAPPY-EVER-AFTER MYTH – Marriage will make me happy forever.**
Women grow up believing in true love and finding their knight in shining armour. He is preferably a handsome, sexy man with a nice car and a good haircut, who will whisk you off to the Caribbean for a beachside wedding and move you into a rose-trimmed cottage where you will live happily ever after. You will be everything to each other and no matter what problems life throws at you, your love and support will get you through.

The truth: You finally get to the altar and heave a huge sigh of 'no more nights alone with the cat' relief. As the years go by, the humdrum grind of work, the school run and the weekly supermarket schlep can chip away at any romantic ideal we hold. Then, when we look over at our farting, snoring beloved – his toe clippings neatly placed on the night-stand – is it any surprise that we get a makeover and run off with the mailman?

**PETER PAN MYTH – I will be young forever.**
Mortgages, DIY and the in-laws all seem like the scariest ride. And breeding? Don't get me started. The age-orexic may be over 40, but you resolutely refuse to act your age. Not for you the slow decline into comfy shoes and Michael Bublé records; you are more likely to be wearing a cartoon T-shirt with your iPod belting out the latest tunes. The idea of set-tling down seems like the end of the road and you are more at home with your Playstation than on the school run.

The truth: There is only so long you can go on hanging out with people in their 20s before you start to look like a wizened old teenager. Whilst you still act like an overgrown tween, deep down you know that the game's up. The trouble is, you don't know any other way to live.

**'PANK' (professional alpha no kids) MYTH – My glamorous job will bring me happiness.**
Climbing the career ladder is exhausting, exhilarating and bound to get you a penthouse in the centre of town. You get to live the dream and that includes first-class travel, cham-pagne at the airport and luxury on tap. No nappy bags and nights of broken sleep for you, you think, as you attend another high-flying meeting in Hong Kong.

The truth: No regrets, you always said. Then one day you start to feel as if something is missing. Oops! You have forgotten to have kids and a family. Suddenly your Italian leather upholstered chair and your 50-inch plasma screen all appear cold and uninviting and you rush off to freeze your last decaying egg, wondering where all the good men have gone.

**DO IT ALL MYTH – I can have a challenging job, look great at a party and manage the children, all with immaculately blow-dried hair and a smile.**
Your home is decorated top to bottom, it has a loft extension and under-floor heating. You manage the children, the artist husband, the nanny, and you still head up a team of 30 at work.

The truth: You are a controlling, Type A personality who is one day going to rush screaming naked down the street in the grip of full-on 'burn out'.

## SO WHAT DOES IT ALL MEAN?

Midlife is that awful moment when you wake up and realise that all the dreams you had when you were young of 'happy ever after', or thoughts that you are somehow different from everyone else, have all been a bit of a dream. And then the big downer – cripes! You're not that young thing any more and you know what? We are all going to die some day.

Midlife is not for wimps!

Here are the six top OMG realities of being a grown-up:

- No, sorry, you're not special. Yes, you may be talented and kind and you can touch your nose with your tongue. Congrats. The truth is, we're all pretty much the same.
- You can't control anything, let alone how your life is going to turn out.
- No one is perfect. We are all just flawed human beings jostling along and trying to be happy.
- No one knows what tomorrow has in store for us – you could be run over by a bus or you could be a Lotto millionaire by breakfast.
- We are all on the slow slide to wrinkly decrepitude and death, and the Stairmaster, botox and holidays in the Tuscan sun are just clever ways of keeping our mind off it.
- Just because you're nice doesn't mean you get to pass Go. Life is not that simple. Bad things happen to good people and vice versa.

## AT THE CROSSROADS

It is not easy. We rail against our dwindling fertility, we stomp our feet as we pluck out another grey hair and we cry as we look at our wrinkles etching themselves across our faces. Midlife is a bit like standing bewildered and battered at a neon-lit crossroads. Behind us is the flippy young girl with the honey-highlighted hair and the dewy skin, and in front of us is a long undiscovered road down which we are just going to get older. Aaargh!

Hang on a minute!

Scared of midlife?

Don't be. It may sound a bit wretched on the outside. But honestly, this loss of our younger self at middle age is entirely natural, and really not as bad as it seems. Instead of seeing it as the arrival of a scary monster with chin hairs and weekly panic attacks, could the middle years be a moment of throw-caution-to-the-wind freedom, where you dance on tables, kayak up the Amazon and pilot your own plane?

This period is a chance to stop and rethink your life. You may have been papering over the cracks of a boring marriage and decide to take a round-the-world, 'journey of discovery' holiday. You may decide to paint your apartment pink for the hell of it, or have hot sex with the gardener. Whatever you do, it is how you decide to live the rest of your life that will make all the difference to how you age.

The middle years are the time to get rid of the old you and discover a whole new improved you. It is never too late to change or make the tweaks that need to be made.

So embrace it as the beginning of an exciting journey, preferably in first class with a glass of champers and a young toy boy by your side. Okay, ditch the TB, but enjoy the ride.

## DROPPING THE FAÇADE

Do you really want to spend the rest of your time on earth hankering after the days when you looked effortlessly lovely? Stop for a minute. You are forgetting that life wasn't always that great. Have a look at some of the ways that we have changed for the better as we have got older.

## THEN

You:

- Tried to please everybody.
- Smiled at people even when you didn't feel like it, and risked ending up loking like a Cheshire cat.
- Cared about what everyone thought. Am I wearing the right skinny jeans,
- are Jesus sandals in or out?
- Would drop anything you were doing to pick up the kids or make your husband a meal, even if you felt like a wet rag with bells on.
- Followed every trend going, which is why you ended up with frizzed hair and listened to Goth music.
- Didn't dare to slurp hot chocolate or fart in bed with your lover.
- Had toe-curling sex and maybe even a few one-night stands.

## NOW

You:

- Please yourself, and that includes eating cereal in bed.
- Only smile when you really feel happy.
- Act disgracefully if you feel like it.
- Give the husband a takeaway when he's got back from picking up the kids.
- Know what you like and what you don't like.
- Have finally learnt how to get what you want without having a meltdown.
- Don't give a fig if you get angry in public.
- Set the sexual agenda.

# MIDLIFE HURDLES

Of course, not everything is plain sailing at midlife. For a start, the finer points of phone apps are lost on us. Young people snicker when you open your mouth, and don't get me started on how you feel about birthdays. There is no magic formula, but we all come across the same midlife hurdles that can stop us in our tracks and make us feel as if we are an ageing wrinkle-saurus, out of synch with the 'yoof' and stuck somewhere in the Bronze Age.

## TECHNO-BABBLE

It makes you feel like you are on another planet. Technology moves so fast nowadays! What with tweeting, Facebooking or simply sharing your favourite blogs, it is a surprise anybody bothers with verbal interfacing (that's chatting) anymore.

The truth is, most of the stuff going on is beyond you anyway. Do you really want to tell all your Facebook friends what you had for breakfast, or the fact that you dig Justin Bieber's new song? No, I thought not. Sometimes it pays to leave some things alone and do what makes you happy.

## BIRTHDAYS

There is nothing like an impending B-day to give you an attack of the 'I'm so old' jitters. After 40, they seem more like millstones than milestones. Unless you are Demi Moore or

Kim Cattrall, who can look good at any age with enough Restylane and pumped-up lips, approaching the big 50 is like hurtling towards something without being able to put on the brakes. On the upside, at least you might get birthday sex.

## TURNING INTO YOUR MOTHER

If there is one thing we never ever think will happen, it is that one day we will turn into our mothers. After all, didn't you rebel against her when you were younger? You'll be going about your daily chores when suddenly, bam! You do something so mother-like it is scary. You know you're turning into your mother when you:
- Start bossing everyone around, including the dog.
- Get the same hairdo.
- Spit on a tissue and wipe your nephew's/son's/grandson's face. Eeeew!
- Tell your husband to pick up his dirty undies from the floor. Now!
- Find yourself using her phrases. 'So what time do you call this?' you say, as you look at your watch. Hellloo!
- Tell your teenage children to 'turn that music down'.
- Catch sight of yourself in a shop window and think, 'What is my mother doing here?'

## PLANNING THE MID-YEAR HOLIDAY IN JANUARY

Why is it that we can't start the year without booking our two-week holiday in a bunker-like flat, including plane tickets, upgraded seats and our welcome package at the three star hotel. Step away from the computer and repeat after me: 'There will always be a holiday on offer'. Do something in the moment.

## GROWING PAINS

It may seem tough to think of time slipping away, but now that we are middle-aged, the rules of engagement have changed slightly. You may want to consider giving up the following things you can't get away with anymore.
- *Acting cute.* Unless you are Goldie Hawn or Meg Ryan, who somehow manage to play the baby card well into their middle age, acting like a helpless child only works if you have the face to match. Tossing your greying hair from

side to side just makes you look like a mad old lady.

- *Wearing a trilby.* Just because Kate Moss and Eva Longoria wear their straw trilbys with micro shorts and kaftans does not mean that you can.
- *Wearing friendship bracelets.* This is something students on their gap year or 10 year-olds do. It is not cool or even casual to tie those multi-coloured leather bracelets around your wrist, even when you are on holiday.
- *Wearing plastic nails and glittery face makeup.* You are not Kim Kardashian.
- *Saying things like 'awesome', 'fierce' or 'talk to the hand'.* This will only high-light just how old and over-the-teenage-hill you are. The youngsters will not appreciate the fact that you are stepping on their territory, dude!
- *Crying at work.* Big girls don't cry, they suck it up and smile. After all, it was bad enough when you shed tears through lipid eyes and full lips. But really, when an older woman cries it just looks as if her face is crumbling faster than a rock face in a windstorm.
- *Wearing skimpy lingerie-style things to the office.* Unless you want to scare the male interns to death, it is better to look cool, covered-up and chic.

Seven things you can still get away with:
- *Age-appropriate streaks.* Think Sarah Jessica Parker. When she was young-er, she was an all-over blonde. Now sassy and sophisticated in her late 40s, she is a 'bronde' – brown hair with a few blonde streaks. This style will lighten up your face without looking like a Californian ageing surfer.
- *Holding an impromptu dinner party where everyone eats off their knees.* It will bring back memories of your student years. Especially if you crank up the old vinyl and invest in some pink beanbags.
- *Getting your legs out.* As long as they are tanned and toned.
- *Drinking beer straight from the bottle.* There is nothing like necking the amber nectar straight from the bottle to give you that feeling of carefree abandon. Obviously it wouldn't do to knock back a brew if you are at a fancy restaurant.
- *Girl-on-girl action at parties.* Actually, this will probably be a first. But if there is one way to get a stuffy old middlie party going it is leaning over and snog-ging your female neighbour. If Madonna can do it at 50, then so can we.
- *Doing the Macarena.* Only if you add lashings of irony.
- *Wearing a hoodie.* As long as it is a posh hoodie – you know, a nice cashmere blue one with fancy writing and a zip-up top is an age-free zone.

## TIME TO GET OUT YOUR INNER GRUMP

One of the things you can get away with when you are over 40 is being grumpy. Whether you are being a sourpuss, feeling a bit down in the dumps, or are a card-carrying anger merchant, having a strop on is a sign that you are finally middle-aged.

And there are a lot of us angry women about. Not surprisingly, we are a lot grouchier than our mothers, who apart from making the husband a gin and tonic and knitting jumpers, didn't have a whole lot of stress to deal with. Fast forward to the 21st century and women today are torn in many different ways at once. There are career ladders to climb, families to nurture, mobiles that ring constantly, emails to read and a gym membership we don't have time to use. As we grit our teeth through each day, it is no surprise that today's middle-aged women are filled with a low-level simmering rage that is eventually likely to explode, like a pressure cooker that has been left on the stove too long.

Midlife anger is different to the 20-something hissy fit, which is most likely caused by a snagged nail or a tiff with her BBF. Midlife anger has built up over the years. Layer upon layer of betrayals and letdowns, and the fact that life has not measured up to our expectations, makes us boil with rage and rant with regularity.

We manage it, deal with it, try to cram it in the box marked 'to do later,' and put on a smile, but somehow our inner rage comes creeping out of the woodwork in all sorts of different guises.

Signs that you are turning into a middle-aged grump include:

- You feel simmering rage if you hear someone slurp their soup next to you in a restaurant. You have half a mind to go up to them and tell them off!
- You get irritated if someone is late for a meeting/coffee. Instead of letting it go, you wish you could cheerfully strangle them, and give them a ticking off when they arrive.
- You complain about your neighbours to the council when they make too much noise. 'So what if you like listening to Bruce Springsteen on full volume? I am trying to get to sleep!'
- You glare at teenagers who spit/shout/cycle down the street.
- You harrumph when the man opposite you on the train is talking a tad too loudly into his mobile phone. Do you really need to know what he and his mistress got up to last night?
- You demand to see the manager when they stop stocking your favourite brand of spaghetti/wine/bread at the supermarket.

- You screech at the television like a monkey on heat every time there is something that gets your goat.
- You ask them to turn the music down in the restaurant. Even if it is Simon and Garfunkel, you can't hear yourself speak.

**Top 10 things that can make us red with rage**
- Being put on hold.
- Being patronised by the doctor's receptionist. Sit down, madame, your turn will come in five days!
- That irritating voice at the automated checkout machine. Yes, I know I have to put the goddamn produce in a bag. Shut up!
- Christmas. The annual festive panic is enough to drive any middle-aged woman into a state of task-driven fury. And we haven't even bought the presents yet.
- Forgetting your pin number for the ATM.
- Having to watch pretty young girls walk around in dresses the size of hankies and get your husband's attention.
- Having to tip everyone, even the Starbucks girl, the pool man, the supermarket delivery man … is there no end?
- Standing behind people who are dithering. Hurry up, will you. Where's a cattle prod when you need one?
- People talking or rustling papers in the cinema. You even say 'Shush!'
- Men telling you you're hormonal because you are getting angry.

## FIVE WAYS TO DEAL WITH YOUR INNER GROUCH

Okay, so there is nothing that is going to turn you into a calm, relaxed type of person who sits cross-legged and listens to birdsong. However, there are a few things that might help.
- Take up boxing and make-believe you are pummelling your partner/boss.
- Have a lovely hot sauna and let all those niggly tensions ease out of you into the flower-scented air. Then harrumph at the receptionist because someone has taken your towel.
- Have an orgasm, preferably with somebody other than yourself.
- Zip the lip. If you feel you are going to have a tizzy in the middle of the bank or a restaurant, count to 10 really slowly and slow down your breathing. You

may find you reconsider screeching at the bank manager.

- Focus on something really nice. Suppose your partner or a friend has done something that's really got you going. Stop and think of something pleasant, such as a time when they bought you a present or made a kind gesture. After all, the best way to kill an anger attack is to focus on the positive.

# Quiz

We are all different, and how we cope with midlife depends on who we are. So why not try our fun quiz and find out what kind of midlifer you are.

**1 What best describes your dress style?**
a) An Abercrombie & Fitch hoodie with a plain T-shirt and skinny jeans.
b) A designer dress with Jimmy Choo stilettos and a kick-arse watch.
c) Tailored suit and briefcase.
d) Smock top and comfy jeans.

**2 Ever since you were a little girl, you have always dreamed of:**
a) Holidays in exotic locations.
b) Having the house of your dreams, better than anyone else's.
c) Having a glittering career.
d) Having the perfect family.

**3 Your ideal man is:**
a) Young.
b) Someone who does what I tell him.
c) Someone who gives me space.
d) Someone who will always protect me.

**4 You are going to a party and you don't know anyone. Do you:**
a) Wear your most outrageous dress to get attention and talk to everyone.
b) Panic – you hate parties because you are not in control.
c) Sidle up to the important people and start to network.
d) Hang onto the arm of your partner – you hate meeting new people.

**5 If you find yourself with a bit of spare time on your hands, do you:**
a) Go out, get hammered and have a kissing session with the cute guy you met last week.
b) Get back to project managing the loft conversion.
c) Prepare for tomorrow's meeting at work.
d) Make some homemade cookies for the children.

**6 If you could go on any holiday, what would it be?**
a) A month-long adventure holiday with like-minded singletons.
b) A beautiful chateau in the south of France that would be the envy of all your friends
c) A luxury hideaway where you can turn off your smart phone for the first time this year
d) A big family holiday in the countryside with a roaring fire and all the relatives.

**7 How good a cook are you?**
a) I can just about boil an egg. Don't get me started on spag bol.
b) Everything I cook I do to perfection.
c) I don't. Take-aways or restaurants.
d) I love cooking warm, nourishing food for family and friends.

**8 I am motivated most in life by:**
a) Having fun and getting a date.
b) Keeping up appearances.
c) Getting what I want.
d) Making my loved ones happy.

**9 My role model is:**
a) Kate Moss.
b) Martha Stewart.
c) Donald Trump.
d) Mother Teresa.

**10 Which of the following personality traits best describe you?**
a) Spontaneous and fun-loving.
b) Dedicated and tenacious.
c) Ambitious and ruthless at times.
d) Compliant and warm.

**Mostly A's: The age-orexic**
You are warm, extroverted and the life and soul of the party, but sweetie, you have never grown up. You may look good and have lots of money to spend on yourself, but if you are not careful you could end up as the oldest teenager in town. Do you find your friends have all moved on with family and responsibility? If so, now is the time to take stock. Whilst

freedom, fun and adventure are all worthwhile things, in the end they are just experiences; now is the time to build something stable and lasting.

## Mostly B's: The domestic diva

You are a highly driven alpha personality. You have to be the best at everything and that includes baking the best cakes for the school fete and rushing off to coordinate a conference call just as they are giving you first prize. Competitive in everything, you 'helicopter parent' your children and drive them to classes whilst talking on the phone to the boss. Slow down, the world will still carry on without you. Let your children develop their own characters and express themselves to you. That goes for your husband as well.

## Mostly C's: Childfree careerist

Another Alpha personality, you have foregone motherhood in favour of a sparkling career and the thrill of breaking the glass ceiling. Having spent most weekends away on conferences oiling the wheels of your ascent to the heady heights of the executive suite you may just wake up one day and wonder what it is all about. Often a job may be fulfilling and exciting, but an expense account will never love you back. Try to step off the treadmill once every now and then and nurture your friendships or make new friends. They say that happiness is about being connected with other people.

## Mostly D's: Desperate housewife

Life has been like an audition for sainthood. You have been planning out your happy-ever-after narrative ever since you turned mummy's nightdress into your wedding gown at the age of 10. You believe that your family's needs take priority, and you will jump through burning hoops just to get their meals ready on time. Be careful; you may forget who you are and what you want. Maybe it is time for you to confront what you want. Try some evening classes, get out on your own and let your husband know that you can live without him. Carpe diem!

# 3.
# WHERE'S THE CRIMSON LIPPY?
## THE MIDLIFE BEAUTY RULES

# HAVE I PASSED MY SEDUCE-BY DATE?

Of course, when it comes down to it, there is one thing that stands out above all other midlife crisis moments.

There is no escaping the fact: ageing is a cruel business when you're female, especially if you have, until recently, relied on your looks. After all, even if you don't have the looks of Alexa Chung or the legs of Gisele Bundchen, you have gone through life being fairly attractive and scrub up well. In short you are used to getting attention from the opposite sex! In your 20s and 30s, even if you stepped out of the door in a T-shirt and jeans, you could still stop traffic if you put your mind to it. Nowadays, things have changed.

There comes a point when you notice that, hang on a minute, no one is looking at me 'in that way' any more. Suddenly you are seized by a terrible fear. Your head-turning days are over. Jaws will never drop again as you stroll along the beach in a mini kaftan and flip-flops.

Even if you can manage to delay the onset of flabby arms and baggy bums, even if you pump lorry-loads of collagen into your cheeks and buttocks, you will never recapture the dewy-skinned prettiness of your 20s and 30s.

## HOW DO YOU KNOW WHEN YOUR SEX KITTEN DAYS ARE DWINDLING?

Here are the top 20 signs that you're SOTS (slipping off the sexometer):

- Men don't smile back at you, even if you are grinning like a Cheshire cat and flipping your hair like a maniac.
- Male shop assistants don't rush to help you like bees round a honeypot when you are staggering in the carpark, laden down with groceries.
- When men ask you for directions or the time, that's what they want. It is not an excuse to get into bed with you, go on a hot date, or even take you for a coffee. Sorry.
- They give your job to someone half your age.
- Female shop assistants shoo you away from the lacy bras and lead you over to the elasticised foundation garments.
- Spandex knickers start multiplying in your lingerie drawer and your bras are more like windbreakers than frilly, lacy numbers.
- You may not want sex, but you want someone to want sex with you – or at least want to grab you from behind and give you a full-on kiss.
- You catch sight of your reflection in a shop window, and for a split second you wonder who that old bag is in the skinny jeans and inappropriately tight

top. Then you realise it's you.
- Men mistake you for a coat stand.
- The guy at the coffee shop calls you 'madame'.
- You've given up counting grey hairs.
- Men are polite to you
- You wear make-up to go to bed.
- Fashion magazines are filled with teenagers weighing less than two pounds!
- Your face pores look like mini moon craters and there are tufty hairs sprouting out of them.

## AGEING IS INEVITABLE.

Top 10 signs you're getting older:
- You need trifocals to read your mobile phone.
- Everything hurts, and what doesn't hurt doesn't work.
- When you do the hokey-kokey, you put your left hip out and it stays out.
- You run out of breath walking downstairs.
- Your memory has more holes than a screen door.
- When they say feel the burn, you don't think exercise, you think heartburn.
- You're in bed by 10 o'clock and wonder why you stayed up so late.
- You suspect your warranty is wearing out.
- Was that the door creaking? No, sweetie, it was just your knees.
- People start to ask you how things were in your day.

## ARE YOU SUFFERING FROM SEX APPEAL FALLOUT?

Remember when Sharon Stone celebrated her 51st birthday party by being photographed topless for *Paris Match*, or any of Madonna's highly embarrassing crotch shots, nipple outings and bottom flashing moments? Whether you are a bored housewife having hot, dirty sex with the gardener or a highly-paid actress who buys a pair of cartoon boobs, today's 40-something woman can find herself flashing the brickie, and wearing a micro mini the moment she spots the window cleaner.

So how can you spot when you are beginning to tip over into desperately-seeking-sex-appeal syndrome?
- You start buying jeans that are at least one, if not two, sizes too small for you.

- You pose coquettishly alongside your identikit teenage daughter...Subtext 'We could be sisters.' You buy matching dresses, shoes, bras – you name it. Remember Jade Jagger, photographed at a trendy London party with her daughters Assisi, 15, and Amba, 12? They all wore mini-dresses and designer heels.
- You post inappropriately sexy photographs of yourself on the internet, half-naked in a jacuzzi.
- You go on the prowl with your daughter and her friends.
- You grab waiters'/ticket collectors'/beach attendants' bottoms – hell, any male's bottom – and grin when he turns round in horror.
- You laugh kittenishly at jokes, and by that I mean any jokes told by a member of the opposite sex
- You dance like a lap dancer at one of those all-night clubs – that is, until you pull a tendon and end up in the hospital emergency department.
- You go to a male strip club with a group of friends and fling your bra onstage while your female friends egg you on.
- You slather yourself with perfume but all you seem to give off is a whiff of 'eau de desperado'.
- You turn into a bling-wearing, cleavage-showing cougar!

## REWRITING THE MIDLIFE RULES

Okay, so you walk into a party and the cute guy in the corner is not salivating like a dog on heat, your thighs have started to look like a road with speed bumps and you forget everyone's name, including your own mum's. But that doesn't mean you have to shuffle through the rest of your life receding into the background with a frown on your face and a big sign saying 'out to pasture'. Sure, you are not going to be that nubile young thing, still up for it 24/7 as you were in your youth, but neither are you the ga-ga granny trailing her bat wings behind her.

Being sexy and seductive is about more than youthful, elastic back skin and the ability to read the tiny print on crisp packets. It's about feeling good to be alive, being happy, and radiating warmth and fun.

Isn't it time to embrace this shedding of the skin around middle age? And rather than treating it as a negative experience, you can learn to love your midlife years.

You are not alone. All around the world women are crossing the divide into 'not young any more', and are finding different ways of redefining what it means to be middle-aged in the 21st century: In short, they are rewriting the midlife rules.

## ANTI-AGEING TIPS

Here are some anti-ageing tips that have nothing to do with creams and potions.

**Get the va va voom.** Walking with swinging hips and general 'attitude' is seen as sexy, no matter what age you are – just think of Sophia Loren and J.Lo. Flexibility is what makes people appear to walk 'young' and you'll find that having a spring in your step makes you feel lighter.

**Get out the giggle pin.** There is nothing more attractive than a woman who is laughing out loud. It lights up her face and acts like a neon sign, flashing: 'I'm a woman who is fun to be around.' Laughter draws people to you, and when you laugh with one another, a positive bond is created. Of course, we can't all feel like Joan Rivers every day, but you can build laughter into your life. Set aside a 'funny' time each day. Read a humorous book, or watch a film you know is guaranteed to make you laugh. Laughter makes you feel great, and leaves you feeling revitalised.

**Gossip galore.** Did you know that having a good old gossip with friends can make you look and feel younger. According to scientists, a regular chinwag with a female friend can reduce stress and anxiety in women. Apparently it is something to do with our cave-woman instincts for sitting around the fire bonding with the other women. Of course, whilst light-hearted gossip can give us the warm glow of friendship, a backstab-athon is just plain cruel.

**Recapture your childlike spirit.** If you want to find your inner playfulness, ditch the grim, I've-had-a-miserable-day frown and access your inner child. Children live entirely in the moment, unburdened by the past or by worries about the future. Do something childlike each day: jump in puddles, play silly games, walk barefoot in the park. Take a new perspective on life and see it not as something you have to deal with, but as a new adventure.

# SECRETS TO LOOKING SEXY OVER 40

## FOUR WAYS TO REDUCE YOUR REAL AGE

Here are a few steps that will keep you looking and feeling good for longer.

**Eat less, live longer.** You are not doing yourself any good when you eat like a glutton and mainline the choccy biscuits every time you feel a bit low. According to Dr Roy Walford from UCLA, middle-aged mice live 20 per cent longer when eased into a restricted calorie diet. The fountain of youth diet of low-fat protein, low-GI carbs and small amounts of sugar not only gives you glowing skin, it sharpens the brain and body.

**Catch up on the ZZZs.** Getting a good night's sleep is one of the best ways to feel refreshed and at one with the world. First of all, make the bedroom cool and calm. It is a known fact that getting the right sleep temperature is key to unbroken sleep. Listen to some relaxing music or read a book and sip some herbal tea, before you slip into the land of nod.

And did you know that sleep is one of the best anti-ageing remedies there is? Taking an afternoon nap is a perfect way to recharge the midlife batteries and smooth out the tired lines in our faces. Set an alarm for 15 to 20 minutes, close your eyes, and try to rest deeply. You don't have to nod off to feel the restorative benefits; just letting your eyes and mind rest will have you feeling refreshed and raring to go in no time.

**Cut the stress with a knife.** When we get stressed, tons of cortisol (a powerful stress hormone) is released into our body and our defence mechanism has to take time out from fighting disease to deal with it. So it makes sense that, if you can, cutting out meaningless stress is going to be good in the long run. For example, don't catastrophise when you mislay your keys or your wallet. Try to be on time so you don't find yourself in a panic for the airport or an important meeting. Don't take stuff personally. After all, the call centre girl on the other end of the phone is only doing her job!

**Eat your fruit and vegetables.** Yes we all know this one, but how many of us actually manage to eat our five portions a day? If you find it difficult to chomp through mountains of lettuce and alfalfa, make a green or fruit smoothie, buy fruit juices and have spaghetti with tomato sauce. They all count towards your daily intake.

## DON'T BE A SUGAR JUNKIE

If there is one thing that will age you faster than a year in the sun, it is too much of the white stuff. Sugar not only plays havoc with your immune system, it is one of the most ageing substances around.

But hang on a minute. Don't we all grab a sugar fix to get us through the day? Whether it is a chocolate bar, a few cookies or ladening spoonfuls of glistening powder into our tea or coffee, sugar is a delicious substance that makes us feel good and boosts our energy levels.

The trouble is sugar is highly addictive. Why? It stimulates a quick burst of the feel-good brain chemical dopamine. So it is no surprise that you want more. The trouble is, you need more to give you the same sensation. Once you start, you can't stop. Result – a rapidly ageing face and cellulite on your derrière.

## KICK THE HABIT

Before you skedaddle off for your next hit, read these four tips to help curb your cravings:

- If you want to go cold turkey, be aware that you will feel rotten for at least a week. And if you have a sweet tooth you will soon be back on the white stuff. The best way to deal with it is not to make sugar a forbidden food, but to allow yourself a little every day.
- Seek out natural highs. Chomping through a crisp apple or slicing off a chunk of juicy pineapple or a slice of sun-drenched mango, are all sweet tooth favourites, without the guilt. They are rich in fructose, a natural sugar, and full of healthy vitamins and super nutrients.
- Don't switch to sugar-free drinks and snacks. Most food labelled sugar-free contains artificial sweeteners and will create a hormonal mess inside. Besides, they stimulate our appetite and make our cravings worse.
- Do the two small squares of chocolate after dinner routine. So many women crave something sweet in the evening, and allow themselves a couple of squares of their favourite chocolate or a couple of sweets. It not only satisfies the craving, it tops off the evening nicely.

# MIDLIFE MIRROR SYNDROME

## Fast fact

Did you know that middle-aged women dislike what they see in the mirror four times more than young women? Research shows that 90 per cent of women in their 40s and 50s are so depressed with their image, they suffer 'Midlife Mirror Syndrome'. Just nine per cent of women over 45 feel proud of what they see in the mirror, compared with the 42 per cent of 20–25 year-olds and 43 per cent of 30-somethings who are happy with what they see.

You are suffering from Midlife Mirror Syndrome if:

- You can't look in the mirror without doing a 'cheek-ometer' – aka, pulling the skin up from around your cheek and pretending you are back in the days of your youth.
- First thing in the morning your face reminds you of a battered old trout with a mop stuck on top of it.
- You hide all the mirrors in the house except the one that makes you look 10 times thinner than you are.
- You are saving your pennies for an eyelift/facelift/brow job.
- You have gone into grooming overdrive. Your bathroom drawers and cupboards look more like a chemist's store cupboard – how many face packs, unguents, white pastes can a girl have?
- Every time you look in the mirror all you hear are the words, 'OMG, you're ugly, look at those bags, those jowls, that double chin. Trowel some makeup on and fast!'

## FLATTER YOUR REFLECTION

Each of us has the power within ourselves to change how we look. If you stare in the mirror and give yourself a stern telling off, you are not only giving yourself a stress attack, you are making yourself older in the process. When your eyes take in something they likes, your brain's reward system is activated and you will see an instant improvement in your face. Look in a full-length mirror and find five things that make you feel good about yourself. Take note of your physical attributes (eyes, lips, hair, legs, smile) and your style (hairdo, clothing, stance, makeup) and concentrate on your good bits.

## STOP COMPARING YOUR LOOKS TO OTHERS'

When you compare your looks to other women you instantly feel like the ugliest woman on the planet. Research shows that friends, acquaintances and even celebrities have a profound effect on how we perceive our appearance. Try to celebrate what is unique about you – after all, you are not in competition with anyone else.

## DO SOME SELF-PERSUASION

If you believe something enough, it becomes a self-fulfilling prophecy, and other people will eventually believe it too. You think you have nice hair/a fun personality/good legs then you will start to act in a more confident, sexy way. Soon you will actually become sexier and more confident.

## MIDLIFE BEAUTY RULES

Grooming cannot put an end to an attack of midlife angst, but it can make it more bearable. If you are going to avoid that slippery slope into invisibility, then there are a few things to embrace in your beauty regime.

**Go glossy.** Nothing packs as much pick-me-up power as clean, glossy hair, manicured nails and fragranced skin. Looking after yourself not only makes you feel better, it says you take pride in how you look and that in itself will make sure your hair is regularly cut and coloured. Forget spending money on expensive blow-dries. The right cut and colour, with regular blow-dries in between, is all you need.

**Fade out the grey**. Going grey may be liberating, but it is also ageing. Reach for the bottle or go to a professional. Either way, highlights will knock at least five years off your age and soften your face to boot.

**Good foundation.** It's a fact: older skin is more uneven, and that is partly what gives midlife women that 'I'm always dog-tired' look. Make a good foundation the mainstay of your morning skin routine. Make sure you pick one that is not too heavy – no one wants the pantomime dame look – but choose one that blends in the uneven tones while also offering a degree of protection against future assaults.

**Get a new look.** Whether it's a dramatic new haircut or putting highlights through your hair, creating a new look or even buying a luscious lipstick, a makeover is a quick way to feel better about yourself. Changing your look or just indulging in a bit of 'me time' can banish feelings of midlife angst.

**Exfoliate.** Come the middlie years, we tend to lose that youthful radiance. So if you want to keep your face looking as fresh as you can, rub away the dead skin cells. After a hard night partying, or as a weekly rule, exfoliate the dead cells that lie on the skin and can make our skin look dull. You can buy cheap exfoliating creams that gently slough away the dead skin cells and leave us looking as fresh as a middlie daisy.

## HOW TO GET SEX-CAT EYES

For instant sex appeal, create sexy eyes. Start with a black or brown eye pencil, and sweep upwards and into a point at the outer corner of the eye. As a finishing touch, apply several coats of mascara.

- When applying mascara, drag the wand outwards to the outer upper corner to open up eyes further.
- Everyone needs some colour in the face. Use cheek creams in peach, pink and berry colours to give yourself a healthy flush.
- Wear a lip gloss in a light pink colour. It amplifies your mouth and gives it a bright appeal, adding instant glamour.

## FIVE THINGS TO GET INTO BEFORE YOU HIT MIDDLE AGE

- Designer specs. After all, have you ever looked at yourself in a pair of $2 jobbies? Frightening, huh?
- A proper bra fitting. Our bodies change as we age, and the last thing you want is to be doing is hoiking up the bra straps when you are out and about at a posh party.
- Having a manicure. Chipped, bitten nails are oh-so-teenage.

- Invisible underwear. Really, a VPL (visible panty line) at your age just looks clumsy.
- Washing off your makeup at night. Yup, panda eyes and crusty foundation is not a good look over 25, let alone 40.

## FIVE THINGS TO GET RID OF BEFORE YOU'RE MIDDLE-AGED

- Scrunchies. You know, those hair-bandy things that make you look like an overgrown teenager at best, or worst a midlifer with zero dress sense.
- Sparkly décolleté – really, there is simply no excuse to look like a Las Vegas showgirl.
- Blue eyeshadow. Yes, it brings out the colour of blue/grey eyes, but it also makes you look like an ageing member of ABBA or just a 70s throwback.
- Bushy eyebrows. Strong eyebrows may be topping off the famous heads in Hollywood, but after a certain age you just look like Groucho Marx.
- Cutting your own hair.

## MIDLIFE HOTTIES

### Julia Roberts (45)

She's a mother, wife and still as hot as can be. Julia's also embracing her mid-years – recent photographs of her on the beach showed that whilst she is exercising to keep her figure, she has avoided the 'starve yourself to a size zero' route.

### Elizabeth Hurley (47)

Lizzie may be getting in a younger model to showcase her own bikini line but that doesn't stop her looking great in leg-revealing dresses, with a cleavage to die for.

### Elle Macpherson (48)

She's the skinny jean, leather-trouser-wearing, ultimate rock chick mum. Okay, so she does tip over into teenage territory sometimes, but with a bod like hers, she manages to get away with it.

### Salma Hayek (46)

She is the smouldering sex siren who manages to combine class with cleavage, and sass with sex appeal.

**Jennifer Aniston (43)**

This tank top wearing midlifer has shown the world that it is possible to look casually sexy in a natural, outdoorsy way.

**Sarah Jessica Parker (47)**

Style icon for most of the 90s, SJP manages to have that rare thing – 'age-appropriate sex appeal'. With her colourful mix of designer clothes and curly 'bronde' (blonde-brunette) hair, she manages to look at once fun and sexy, with overtones of kooky just for good measure.

**Madonna (54)**

Okay, so no one could match Madge with her four hours a day exercise regime, and her diet of one grape a day. But the Madonna appeal is less about her iron glutes and skinny physique and more about her can-do, 'no one gets the better of me' attitude.

**Kim Cattrall (56)**

Sophisticated, with that creamy, sexy voice, Kim is a sex kitten who is determined to keep on purring.

## THE KINDEST CUT

A word on cosmetic surgery. When it comes to improving on Mother Nature, going under the knife is your choice. For some people the idea of doing something that could make you feel a lot better about yourself is a no-brainer. For others, the very thought of 'turning back the clock' surgically is scandalous. If you are deliberating over whether to slice away the years, here are some things to consider.

- If you are going for the facelift, never listen to anyone who says you don't need it or will look like a human wind tunnel. If you want it, go ahead.
- Whatever you decide to have done, research is the key.
- Find a reputable surgeon, one with appropriate qualifications. These can all be found on the internet and verified. You don't want to fall victim to a cosmetic cowboy.
- Be clear about what you want. Some unscrupulous surgeons may try to sell you more procedures than you need. So much so that you may end up with the face of a 20 year-old, and the second mortgage to go with it.
- Don't skimp on after care, such as bed rest and sleeping with your head

propped on the pillow. The body wants to heal itself and if you get up and start dancing around the sitting room, you will only delay the process.

- Decide whether you want to come clean or keep it under wraps. Joan Rivers likes to tell the world her beauty 'secrets', and there is much to be said for coming clean. It stops any of the has-she-or-hasn't-she gossip. On the other hand, maintain the illusion and say you are going on vacation for a while. Stay tucked up indoors until the swelling has gone down and you feel ready and rejuvenated to go outside.

- When people tell you how wonderful you look, you just smile and say, 'St Lucia was simply amazing.'

## FILL ME UP, SCOTTY

A lot of women are queasy about surgery and prefer to plump from within. Facial fillers such as collagen and Restylane can smooth and reconfigure the face without you having to go under the knife. If you want to avoid conditions such as 'bat brow' (a startled look from too much botox) and bumpy skin, you really need to do your research. Permanent anti-ageing fillers can be administered by unregulated practitioners, so make sure you go to a reputable doctor, even if it does cost more. You don't want to end up with the following:

- Ping-pong face – this is when they inject too much filler into the face and you end up with lumps like ping-pong balls under the skin!

- Trout pout – this occurs when the surgeon injects too much filler into the lips. It is quite common with overenthusiastic celebrities who are desperate for lips like Angelina Jolie, only to end up with a mouth like a fish.

# Quiz

We may be midlifers, but that doesn't mean the party's over yet. Do our fun quiz and find out if you are sliding into granny grump territory or if you still wanna party like its 1999.

**1 When at a party, what are you most likely to be doing?**
a) Looking at your watch. It's already 9.30.
b) Chatting away to close friends.
c) Dancing and knocking back the tequila.

**2 What is likely to be found in your pocket or purse?**
a) Tissues and a Bandaid.
b) Breath mints.
c) Lip gloss and mascara.

**3 If you were going shopping, what would you prefer to buy?**
a) A practical gadget for the kitchen.
b) A nice warm jumper that you can wear every day.
c) A slinky dress for yourself.

**4 Which is the most true for you?**
a) I have hidden all the mirrors in the house.
b) I only have a mirror in the bathroom.
c) I have a mirror in every room.

**5 Your idea of a good party is:**
a) I don't party. I prefer watching a box set with my loved one.
b) A dinner party with old friends.
c) A full-on, dance-your-hearts-out-till-dawn shindig.

**6 If you could be doing any one of these, which would you choose?**
a) Watching TV.
b) Going for a long walk with your partner/friends.
c) Swimming naked in the ocean.

**7 How often do you smile and laugh each day?**
a) I don't smile or laugh much, it gives you wrinkles and frown lines.
b) I don't laugh a lot but I do smile and I mean it.
c) I am a laugh a minute and smile at strangers, even on the train.

**8 How often do you play the fool?**
a) Never, only idiots make a fool of themselves.
b) When I'm around children I can let myself go a bit.
c) Whenever I feel like it. I find having a funny view of life makes me feel good.

**9 How often do you watch funny films?**
a) Never. I would prefer to settle down to a good documentary.
b) Sometimes. I prefer action or thriller movies, though.
c) Frequently. There is nothing more de-stressing than a good belly laugh.

**10 Someone comes to you crying. Do you:**
a) Tell them you are too busy and will talk to them tomorrow.
b) Give them some advice, but wish you were a million miles away. You find these kinds of conversations difficult.
c) Put your arm around them and tell them not too worry, that things will get better, and then take them for a coffee.

**Mostly A's:** You take yourself and life quite seriously, and find yourself on the outside of the fun crowd. Try loosening up a little bit – do or say something silly. You may find that if you throw caution to the wind, you will actually enjoy yourself.

**Mostly B's:** You are great at being sensible, and although you can enjoy yourself, you seem quite hung up on this being middle-aged thing. So we are over 40. Sometimes we just have to seize the moment and be spontaneous. Good luck.

**Mostly C's:** You are the life and soul of the party and you are not ready to hang up your streamers yet. Probably an extrovert with a warm heart, midlife has not managed to curb your enthusiasm or disconnect your funny bone! Keep on partying.

# 4.

# STRAPPY SANDALS AND DANGLY EARRINGS

## KNOW YOUR MIDLIFE STYLE

Let's not kid ourselves. Does that see-through micro mini you used to wear to parties now just look like desperately-seeking-attention syndrome? Will the skimpy shorts and flip-flops that look great on a winsome 19-year-old make you appear as if you are mad, sad and trying too hard?

Sure, we all want to continue to get attention at some level. After all, it feels good when we get a glance from the hot guy standing at the bus stop, or a compliment from an old friend at a party. And you can still rock the skinny jeans/Converse combo, or look sassy in a pair of wide-legged trousers and a turtle-necked sweater.

What you don't want is to think you are the same person you were 20 years ago.

The trouble is, nowadays making the transition from your porn-chic 20s to your fabulous 40s without coming a cropper is not always easy. Aren't we still mesmerised by the skinny red leather trousers currently in vogue? Or grappling with the 'can we still wear thin spaghetti straps' question?

That's the problem. We are not sure what 40-plus looks like any more. Even though you can buy and wear what you want, and even If you've got the figure to squish into a Hervé Léger dress, it doesn't mean it looks good or that it is age appropriate. Is there anyone who thinks Madonna (54) looks hot to trot in ripped leggings and disco leotards? Or Christie Brinkley (58), all sinewy-armed in her tight bandage dresses?

It wasn't always like this. Years ago, our mothers' generation knew the dress code. Come middle age, they slipped dutifully into twin sets, house dresses and sensible shoes. Nowadays, women have a lot more style choices. We can shop at the same stores as our daughters, skinny jeans are for all ages, and wedge boots are a must for anyone who thinks they are fashion forward.

Getting it perfect in your 40s is not always easy, but the first step is to know when the face and the fashion simply don't match.

## YOU'RE IN DENIAL IF:

- You're trying on bright swirly-print trousers and gladiator boots.
- Everyone else in the changing room looks half your age.
- You think that over-the-knee socks and shorts is a good look for you.
- You think you can still wear a ballerina dress complete with pink tulle.
- You are still rocking over-the-knee boots.
- You think you look like a rock chick with tousled hair and heavily kohled eyes.
- You have a belly button piercing, or worse, a tongue piercing.

- You think neon is the perfect way to brighten up your complexion. It won't.
- Your fashion role model is Rhianna.
- You're thinking of gettting a tattoo.
- You have size blindness and are still buying those too-tight mini dresses.

## FIVE MISTAKES WOMEN MAKE

Midlife dressing is a minefield. It may be tempting to try to hold back the years and claw back some of your dewy-skinned youth, but clothes should make us look more attractive than when we are naked, not less. Wanting to look 15 years younger than your actual age has a faint whiff of desperation. Here are some of the mistakes that women make:

- **16/61 syndrome.** Whereby a woman looks like a pert-bottomed, bouncy-haired young thing from behind and a grandmother from the front. Not only will you look like you are trying too hard, it gives the impression that you are not comfortable with who you are.
- **Baring your midriff.** No, no, no! After all, unleashing middle-aged flesh onto the world is simply not fair, and not pretty. Even if you are as flat as an ironing board, wanting to show the world that you do 15,000 sit-ups a day is just showing off. And yes, even Madonna looks like a crumbly teenager when she stuffs her midlife bod into black leggings and tiny Tees.
- **Being fashion roadkill.** Don't wear spray-on, over-the-knee boots and black leather fingerless gloves – the hard-edged, rebels-only kind – along with miniskirts, short shorts and strapless vests thateven the celebs can't carry off anymore. This includes squeezing yourself into tight leopard-skin dresses and studded stilettos.
- **Comparing yourself to you in your 20s.** It is a fact that few people look as attractive in middle age as they did when they were bright young things. Taking a walk down memory lane and trying to recreate your younger self is going to make you a) depressed and b) have a full-on identity crisis. The goal is to look as good as you can for your age and recognise that your body and your face are ageing.
- **Showing too much flesh.** Always remember the rule of one. If you are going to wear a strapless top (great if you have killer arms) don't wear a miniskirt. And if you have the legs to go short, whatever you do, resist the high heels; that is strictly for the girls.

# DO'S AND DON'TS OF MIDLIFE FASHION

Midlife fashion is still a maze of rules and regulations, so check these do's and don'ts of dressing your age:

**Do** learn to love the black opaques. As well as concealing any chicken skin or lumpy legs, black tights automatically make dresses look more chic.

**Don't** wear red, orange or plum coloured tights. They are a young girl's game. And patterned? Don't even go there.

**Do** wear denim skirts. Mid-thigh (if you have good legs) or above-the-knee A-line denim skirts, worn with wedges or biker boots, can make you look youthful and fun, without going down the 'mutton dressed as lamb' route.

**Don't** wear puffed sleeves. Ever. At worst they will make you look like a character in a panto, at best you will look mumsy and blowsy and age you 10 years.

**Do** wear wide-legged trousers. They slim the silhouette, make the legs look longer and have panache. Think Katharine Hepburn, Annie Hall and the cast of the TV series *Charlie's Angels*. Wear with a slim-fitting top to avoid looking baggy all over. A V-necked sweater with a plaid shirt is very retro 70s.

**Don't** ever wear bottom-skimming denim shorts. Revealing this amount of flesh is a clear sign that you are in the grip of a crisis.

**Do** wear biker boots. They are comfy, flat and can toughen up floaty floral dresses and give you an added air of slouchy cool.

**Don't** go the Ugg boot route – like most uncomplimentary fashions, they only look good on girls under 20.

**Do** wear off-the-shoulder dresses and tops. Baring your shoulders, back and collarbone is sophisticated and gently sexy without looking desperate.

**Don't** get the cleavage out unless it looks really, really good. Over a certain age the big cleavage look is sartorial car crash material.

# THINGS THAT LOOK DAFT AFTER 40

- Sparkly hot pants – they may have looked good in your disco days but leave it to the young ones.
- Ditto boob tubes and leotards – leave them at Studio 54.
- Ra-ra skirts of any length. You may have worn them back in the 80s with cropped Tees and pirate boots, but now they just look as if you are mad.
- Harem pants or any trousers where the crotch hangs around the knee area.

Do you really want to look like you are wearing a giant nappy?

- Leggings – unless under a dress or tunic – will make your legs look like sausages wrapped in cling film.
- White frilly dresses. You are not auditioning for a part in *Little House on the Prairie.*
- Jimjam fashion. Even if you are just popping out for milk in the morning, the fashion for wearing your pyjamas out in the street à la Sarah Jessica Parker only looks good if you are very young or very famous.
- Laddered tights – unless you are Rhianna or any other hot young celebrity, the holey tights under shorts or miniskirt look is strictly for grungy teens who wear them with workman's boots and rail about the status quo.
- Ultra-tight jeans that show oodles of splodgy overhang.
- Jumpsuits. Unless they are non-clingy and worn with high heels, you will end up looking like a racing car driver, or worse, Elton John circa 1975.
- Crocs. These bulbous, brightly-coloured clogs have taken over the feet of middle-aged men and women alike. So what if they last forever and are the most comfortable thing you have ever worn? They are the footwear from hell and only good on the under 10s.
- Those halterneck dresses that plunge way south of the naval. Think J.Lo in that patterned Donatella Versace number.

## YOU'RE TOO YOUNG FOR:

- Long cardis that hide the backside. It only adds bulk and sends out the message 'I am so insecure about my body I want to cover it up'.
- Orthopaedic sandals. Save them for the care home.
- Patterned scarves slung nonchalantly around the neck – you are not a politician's wife.
- Pop socks with sandals. Again, really?
- The dress-with-coat ensemble. Too pristine, too outfitty and far too co-ordinated.
- Pussycat bows and pie-crust collars. They weren't even sexy in the 80s.
- Voluminous skirts that age you 10 years.
- Baggy clothes that cover up your curves.

# MIDLIFE STYLE STRATEGY

If you really want to nail midlife style, you need an overall strategy, one that manages to connect with who you are and where you are in your life.

So follow the middle life style rules and you can still be fabulous and 40.

## DE-AGE YOUR WARDROBE

Five simple rules that will help you turn back the ageing clock:

- Work the accessories. A statement bag, a simple necklace or a pair of accent gloves can keep your outfit on trend.
- Keep the hemline short. Mid-calf may seem safe, but it will shorten your legs and look frumpy. A skirt just above the knee will slim your figure and elongate your legs.
- Add a shoulder pad if your shoulders are sloping. Any kind of droop will make you look heavier than you are. Adding breadth to the shoulders will add definition and take pounds off your hips.
- Don't wear anything that strains the seams of your clothes. Clothes that drape the body – jersey or anything with lycra in it – will make you look younger and more feminine.
- Buy a new bra. Hoiking up bra straps, walking around with splurging back fat, or experiencing too much jiggle factor means one thing – you need to upgrade your underwear. As we get older our shape, thickness and yes, our breasts, change, so it may be that the bras you wore 10 years ago are way too small or even too big. Go to a lingerie department and get a proper bra fitting – it will take 10 years off you.

## PRACTI-FASHON

As we get older, we want clothes that suit our work–life balance and look good at the same time. Practi-fashion is about looking polished and chic whilst trying to navigate the weather, the kids, the job and stay comfortable.

Five things that bridge the gap between comfort and style.

- The grown-up hoodie. We all want the cosiness of leisure wear, without looking like a gang member. Cue the posh hoodie. Stylish in cashmere or soft cotton, they are comfy, cosy and chic, and can be worn with dresses, jeans or even a smart pair of trousers.

- Ankle cowboy boots. These hybrid boots are comfortable to walk in and yet avoid the 'I wanna be a cowboy' schtick.
- The posh rain boot is a great way to combine practical with country chic. The rubberised mock-croc effect fashion rubber boot is part fashion/part practical defence against mud, and they look so good, they can even be worn with skirts and dresses.
- Quality sports-urban wear. Soft Luxe Tee shirts with long sleeves and beautiful cashmere tracksuit bottoms are far too chic and expensive to wear to the gym, and are perfect for casual daywear.
- Wedges. These are the perfect way to get height without the bunions and 'I can't walk another step' sore feet. Design-wise they are on trend and can make a pretty dress look edgy.

## STEP-BY-STEP GUIDE TO GETTING MIDLIFE CHIC

Let's face it, you no longer have the freedom to wear exactly what you want as you did in your 20s. Back then, a baggy T-shirt with a scruffy miniskirt, flip-flops and ropey hair managed to look chic in a thrown together hippie way. Back then you could get away with multi-coloured jumpers, bright coloured leggings and high-top trainers and still look wacky and fun. If you wear clothes like that now, people are more likely to think you are an eccentric bag lady and cross to the other side of the street.

The key to midlife style is not about looking bang on trend or cutting edge, it is simply learning what works for you.

## CLASSIC STYLE

This is a perfect midlife formula. A favourite with style icons such as Grace Kelly, Jackie Onassis and Natalie Portman, this look has always been grounded in versatile basics and accessories. Sleek and elegant, it is hard to mess up if you play by the rules.

### Get the look

- Avoid clutter. Ruffles or other fashionable detailing that you think might brighten up an outfit can make you look heavier and add years to your age.
- Say no to layering, or anything that is baggy or saggy. Structured looks are better as we age as they sharpen up the silhouette.
- Use prints sparingly. Loudness isn't classic, so if you love prints, keep them quiet. The focus should be on the garment's shape – simple stripes, pretty

florals, small polka dots. Avoid glaring geometric shapes or swirly patterns.

- Stick to solid neutrals. The key colours are camel, black, white, navy, cream and grey. Pink goes well as long as it is not that glaring fuchsia so beloved of politicians' wives. If you want to add colour, such as bright orange, get a statement bag.

## Style pros

- Is reliably chic, perfect for events when you are unsure of the dress code.
- Creates a pared-down silhouette that is unmistakably chic and alluring, as well as slimming to the figure.

## Style cons

- Worn wrong, classic can look a bit uptight and formal. If you are doing the white shirt, undo a few buttons and flash a lacy bra. Glam up an outfit with outrageous shoes such as silver sandals or death-defying stilettos.
- It is not the most imaginative of looks, but that's the point really.

## Classic pieces

- **Well-cut jeans.** Preferably dark. Faded denim is a bit of a 70s throwback.
- **Sleek black turtleneck.** This is a versatile classic that can be worn with everything. It adds instant sophistication when worn with jeans and a pair of Jackie Onassis sunglasses, and smart sex appeal when combined with a tweed pencil skirt and stilettos.
- **The shift dress.** A celebration of understated elegance and classic chic. Whether worn with turbocharged stilettos or a simple pair of ballet flats, the shift always manages to make the wearer stay the sophisticated side of sexy. Invest in a classic LBD (little black dress) if you want a perfect mix of 'look at me' and classic cool.
- **The pencil skirt.** Gives an outfit an element of dressed-up chic that no pair of trousers ever can. The high-waisted, long line shape wraps itself around the hips and thighs, and creates an instant curvy silhouette that is both sexy and elegant.
- **The wrap dress.** The 'go anywhere' dress for the busy woman about town. Body conscious but unconstricting, it is forgiving to thighs and tums and is universally flattering.

# GROWN-UP GLAM

Just because we don't look like Beyoncé or J.Lo doesn't mean that glam is off the style menu. For the big event – a showy wedding, or a black tie do – nothing feels better than looking drop dead gorgeous. And anyone can be glamorous with enough know-how and a pair of spandex knickers. The trick of grown-up glamour? Think of those corsets, scratchy beads and skyscraper stilettos: it is the willingness to put up with a bit of discomfort to look womanly and sexy.

## Get the look

- Stay clear of the gimmicks: too much cleavage, thigh high splits (unless you're Liz Hurley) or anything mini. The trick to grown-up glamour is to stop short of a full-on trend and focus on a few key ideas that can update any outfit. Invest in a pair of large 70s-style sunglasses. They not only hide the bags and create intrigue, they are the best short cut to Jackie Onassis style glamour.
- Buy quality. Throw-away chic is strictly for women who look good in a bin-bag liner, aka anyone under 20.
- Don't be scared to shimmer. No one said you can't do gold lamé like Marilyn Monroe, just make sure that the dress is not the size of a hankie and is well cut. After all, you want to look elegant and a bit out of the ordinary, not like Jessica Rabbit's auntie.
- The red dress. Simple, strong and far too modern to be coy, wearing red is a guaranteed head-turner at any age.
- If you are going to wear that multi-coloured Versace number with a pink cardigan and gold shoes, you have got to make sure you can carry it off. Wearability is key to looking glamorous in midlife.
- If you are wearing a flamboyant dress, don't go overboard on the jewellery, or the shoes. They will give you a distinct whiff of mutton dressed as lamb. Ditto fur wraps and pink pashminas.

## Style pros

- Looking glamorous is the perfect way to pull you out of your everyday' life. Remember that what you wear affects the way you feel, the way you move and even the way you think. A way of looking becomes a way of being.
- Done properly, it is a guaranteed way to get you attention and will make sure you are not ignored at parties or dinners.

## Style cons

- Confidence is key when putting yourself in the limelight. So don't risk full-throttle glamour if you are having a bad day.
- Glam style is not that big on comfort, so if you are not in the mood to spend all evening squished into a pair of spandex knickers or tottering on five-inch platforms, give it a miss and pull on a tried and trusted jeans and floaty top combo.

## Glam garments

- **The beaded dress.** Glamour needs to be noticed. Serious beading is full-on glamour and the sparkle will draw attention to you in a nanosecond. Not only that, it will lighten up your face, making it look younger. There are a lot of beaded dresses on the market, so make sure you go for one with structure.
- **The corset dress.** Provocative, sexy and curve enhancing, the corset dress is the perfect bombshell outfit. Based on the traditional girdle, it pulls and pushes to give you the drop dead curves of a 50s siren. You will be feeling like Marilyn in no time.
- **The trouser suit.** In an edgy cut with a cleavage-hugging jacket, the trouser suit in black or white radiates instant glamour with grown-up attitude. Elle Macpherson and Demi Moore love their tuxedos. Make sure that it skims the body but is not overly tight. Go for a strategic camisole for a hint of modesty.
- **The evening gown.** This one makes a huge statement. Vintage glamour is perfect for such a show-stopper. Go for a 30s look with a draped structured dress that cinches in the waist and lifts the cleavage. Sexy and decidedly grand.
- **The divaesque top.** If you are strictly a jeans-with-everything lady, then glam up your outfit with a glamorous top. Either a flamboyant jacket in a bright colour or a shimmery tank with beaded detail at the collar will work wonders. Add a beaded clutch for instant sparkle.

# HOW TO BE A LEATHERETTE AND LOOK FOXY

How old can you be and still pull off leather? If you want to avoid looking like a rebel without a waistline, follow our age-appropriate rules.

There's no more potent statement for a woman than wearing leather. It is a symbol that can send out all kinds of messages — ladylike and sexy, glamourpuss or just elegant and rich. But if you don't want to channel the 'cougar goes sharking' look, then age-appropriate styling is essential. To avoid looking like you're in the grip of a full-blown midlife crisis, take our tips on how to get your leather into gear.

## LEATHER TROUSERS

Nothing can cause quite as much of a stir as a pair of sexy, well-fitting leather trousers. It is almost as if the moment you put them on, you go from 'mum in the kitchen' to 'girl on a motorbike' look.

Avoid ultra-skinny leather trousers that have jegging status. After all, you don't want to look like you're wearing spray-on legs, and they are bound to go baggy and saggy in the knees after one wear. Don't wear them with a tight corset top unless you want to look like Ivana Trump or a cougar on heat.

Instead, find a a pair of leather trousers with a trouser-like waistband and proper trouser detailing. Keep them close-fitting without being too tight. For a start, they won't look as MILF-y as the spray-on variety, and no one will accuse you of trying to look like Kate Moss. Wear with a big sweater or T-shirt and bouclé cardigan for slouchy chic.

## LEATHER JACKET

Avoid leather biker jackets at all costs. Unless you want to look like an extra from the film *The Wild One*, hard-core leather jackets are the cornerstone of rockers, rock chicks and rebels, and a midlife no-no.

Instead, go for a smarter look and invest in a soft, blouson-style jacket. They are great over flowery dresses or skinny jeans and can still give you an aura of bad girl cool without the hard edge.

## LEATHER SKIRT

Avoid black second-skin skirts. They are borderline hooker and/or ageing punk rocker. Go for A-line skirts in muted colours to avoid any whiff of sluttishness. A high-waisted pencil midi skirt with a short slit up the back for ease of movement is the ideal compromise.

## HOW TO LOOK GOOD IN HIGH HEELS

The time comes when we have all had enough of our flats, battered Converse or beloved Birkenstocks, and long to totter about on a pair of strappy, flutey-heeled stilettos. The thing is, if you are used to slouching around in sensible flats, then heels can be tricky – but doable.

Here are the golden rules of wearing high heels:

- Calf raises. Always perform this exercise before stepping out in heels as it warms up the muscles that will be used. Standing with your feet flat on the floor, hold on to the back of a chair and slowly lift and lower your heels (10 raises with both, then 10 on the right, 10 on the left).
- Good posture is key if you don't want to hobble around like Tony Curtis in *Some like it Hot*. Open up the shoulders and hold the chin at the correct height. Imagine you have a book on your head, and look straight ahead.
- Take small steps. Place the centre of your foot on the floor, and only when the back foot is coming off the ground should you begin to move your weight forward.
- Relax the knees as you walk and let your hips undulate. Glide through the movement rather than strut like a peacock, and this will give you the unmistakable sashaying wiggle that made Marilyn Monroe so famous.
- Swing your arms and keep your eyes off the floor. Never rush in heels. Nothing looks more sexy and sassy than a woman who takes her time.

## ANIMAL PRINTS

Animal prints – leopard, snake, or whichever animal you're channelling at the moment – are one of the trickiest midlife fashions to get right. Worn wrong, they can hover perilously between ageing cougar and barmaid with a perma-tanned cleavage.

If you want to go wild and avoid looking like mutton, then follow our tips for looking chic in the jungle:

- Leopard-print heels or flats are entry-level animal print for the terrified and manage not to overdo the 'flash cat in the jungle' look. Ditto animal print bags, which are great to add a touch of pattern to a monochrome wardrobe.

- Swathing yourself in a leopard-print scarf is one way to avoid print overkill.
- Whatever you go for, classic 'less is more' works best when it comes to big game. Go for just one jungle item or else you will look like Jackie Collins on a bad night out.
- A leopard-print cocktail dress worn with nude shoes and a beige fitted cardigan or trench coat is one way to pull off the jungle look and keep it the right side of feminine chic.

# MIDLIFE SHOPPING

For midlife women, shopping can often turn from a pleasurable and satisfying experience into an orgy of self-pity and loathing. It only takes the disapproving look of one creamy-skinned sales assistant, or the realisation that the twinkly gossamer slip dress that we saw in *Vogue* makes us look like a panto dame, to reduce us to floods of hormonal tears.

If you want to make sure your shopping trip is a success and not a sob-fest follow these tips.

## SHOPPING CHECKLIST

- Before you set out, take a long, hard look at your existing wardrobe and make a list. Do you need any new jumpers, trousers or shirts? What do you want to update your wardrobe? These are just questions, but they will help you avoid 'impulse buy' syndrome. You know, that thing that overtakes sane women when they see a ludicrously expensive and outrageous pair of pink designer jeans that are going to make them look like ageing candy floss.
- The midlife mantra should be, 'buy less, buy better', which means not rushing off to the first high street store and bringing back bags full of clothes that won't survive one wash.
- Have a budget and stick to it.
- The best shopping buddy is an old, trusted friend. The one you've known long enough that they will tell you, no, you can't wear tiered skirts any more, but won't be jealous when you look better in the faded jean jacket.
- Never take a man. After all, to them shopping is a function: organised, de-

cisive, focused and lasting 10 minutes if you're lucky. Besides, if you insist on dragging them off the sofa/from the computer, they will either moan, fall asleep or worse, check out the snake-hipped shop assistant.

- Watch out for 'fake flattery shop assistant' syndrome. For a start, they are paid to say you look fab in those leopard-skin leggings you were trying on for a joke. As much as you want to think the floaty tea dress looked like it did when you were younger, that is what your sensible friend is for – to act as your purchase filter.
- Never shop with someone younger, prettier or slimmer. You will immediately think you are uglier, older or bigger than you really are, end up gorging on three-layer fruit cake and a double-choc cappuccino, and will feel guilty all weekend.

# 5.
# HOW TO BE
# FIT AT FORTY

## THE MIDLIFE EXERCISE PLAN

Are you driven to despair by the sight of your wobbly underarms in a sleeveless dress? Do you wail at the size of your butt in a bikini? Don't worry, you are definitely not alone. Splodgy bits in areas you had never thought possible are all part of growing up.

Whilst you can go through your 20s and 30s never really thinking about weight or calorie counting, the moment you cross over into middlie territory, boom! Looking and feeling good become issues you have to deal with.

Midlife marks the death knell of that heady time when you can eat deep-fried Mars bars, drink tequilas and smoke cigarettes and still bounce back the next morning looking and feeling as fresh as a daisy. Now, your jeans are so tight they are causing you circulatory problems, hair starts to spring out on the backs of your thighs, lips and chins, and a hangover keeps you in bed all day long.

The truth is the body starts to take a siesta as we hit middle age. Our metabolism, which was racing along nicely, starts to splutter and slowdown like a clapped-out motor car, and things like bum knees and tricky backs become a daily occurrence.

That's the bad news.

The good news is you don't have to panic. Looking and feeling good is easier now than it has ever been. Come middle age, how we look and feel all depends on how we take care of ourselves and how we think. If we eat our goji berries and don't skip breakfast, if we make sure we take regular exercise and get lots of shuteye, our middlie body can stay stronger and fitter for a lot longer than most people think.

And that doesn't mean you have to morph into a long-limbed blonde with perfect proportions, a hand-span waist, perky breasts and honey-coloured skin. After all, why would a 45-year-old woman want to look 25 years old?

Just because celebrities and models think that ageing is a bizarre disease doesn't mean the rest of us have to succumb to the 'bikini fit at 40' pressure. Celebrities are weird fitness freaks known to live off calorie-strict salads, do thousands of sit-ups and go to bed at seven. Their looks are their calling card and their mantra is to stay looking girlie and frisky well into their 90s. Good luck to them.

For the rest of us, the big question we should be asking ourselves is not 'How can I be an eternal teenager with a size zero bod and a penchant for carrying miniature dogs around in my handbag?' but 'Am I fit for my age?' This is crucial, because as our body changes, we need to change how we look after it.

Of course in the 21st century, with its mod cons, convenience food and round the clock entertainment, it's so tempting to sit on your backside and watch another episode of *The Good Wife*, whilst tucking into a packet of chips dipped in chocolate.

And even if we do set ourselves an exercise plan, when it comes to actually doing some sport, we can easily convince ourselves of a million and one reasons why we shouldn't be dragging ourselves out of bed at 6am and trotting off bleary-eyed to the gym. Before you know it, weeks have gone by, your gym kit is still lying unworn on the chair, and you haven't lost a single ounce.

Here are the top 10 excuses middlies use to get out of doing exercise:
- I've got a terrible hangover and need to lie down on the sofa with a cold compress, a DVD and a box of choccies by my side.
- I can't leave the kids home alone – okay, so I know they're teenagers.
- Not today darling, I've got a head/knee/back ache.
- It's raining/cold/windy.
- I haven't got the right gear.
- My favourite program has just started on the television.
- I just ate.
- I'm too fat.
- I'm too tired.
- It's far too early in the morning.

## TOP 10 WAKE-UP CALLS FOR WANTING TO LOSE WEIGHT

Sometimes even the most enthusiastic of us need a bit of help when it comes to getting motivated. There is nothing like your slimmer/younger friend's wedding to make you prise yourself off the sofa, pull on your Lycra tracksuit and go for a run, a walk or to the gym.

Have a look at these top 10 'kick up the backside' triggers we need to focus the mind to getting fit:
- There's a wedding coming up, and it's yours.
- There's a wedding coming up and you're newly single.
- Your friends are all thinner than you.
- You have just split your favourite trousers.
- Your husband has left you for a skinnier model.
- Your underarms flap wildly in the wind every time you wave or clap your hands.
- You've got a school reunion in one month and you've put on one stone since you were a 20-something.

- You're going on holiday with your husband's younger friends.
- You've turned into a couch potato.
- You get out of breath when you run up the stairs.

# MIDLIFE MAINTENANCE PROGRAMME

## STOP THE SPREAD

If you have spent your youth lounging around doing the odd push-up and the occasional jog round the block, it is not the end of the world. It is never too late to get fit and toned. And it doesn't mean you will have to spend the rest of your life getting up at dawn and performing a thousand squat thrusts before downing a glass of warm water and carrot juice for breakfast. Getting fit and toned in midlife is about incorporating some kind of exercise into your busy routine as often as you can.

Here are five easy steps to get you started:

- **Find what works for you and stick with it.** If you don't know what you like, take the time to try some different sports/exercise regimes. Join a yoga or Pilates class, try spinning, Zumba or maybe some light weight training. Even moving around more and going for a walk is a start.
- **Set small goals.** There is no point pinning a picture of Jessica Ennis or Maria Sharapova on your wall and saying 'I want that figure now!' Unrealistic goals are overwhelming and when you don't manage them, you simply go back to watching DVDS on the sofa and eating tubs of ice-cream because you're so depressed. Aim to walk for half an hour three times a week. Whatever it is, make it something that you can manage and that fits in with your life.
- **Pin a big notice on your fridge.** Whether it is to fit into your 'skinny' jeans or simply to tone up your arms, if you write it down, it makes it seem more real, and you are more likely to stick with the program.
- **Try not to be overly critical about yourself.** We all have things we hate about ourselves. Focus instead on how many barbells you have managed to hoik above your head or the number of laps you have swum in the pool.
- **Get an exercise buddy.** Having someone to train with will make it fun and easier to stick to. If it worked for Gwyneth and Madonna, then why not you? And there is nothing like having someone ring your doorbell and drag you off the sofa to go on that run you have circled on your calendar.

## EASY DOES IT

Come middle age, we may like to take things down a notch or two. Incorporating some sort of relaxing activity such as yoga helps us to slow down in this fast-paced modern world. Besides, for ages now New Age junkies have been telling us that bending your limbs into positions called the downward dog, and doing things called throat locks and sun salutations, is the way both to a spiritual nirvana and a toned, lithe body. If the idea of this ancient, twisty health regime appeals to you, then get a little blue roll-up mat and head off to a yoga class.

Of course, all the different types of yoga on offer are enough to confuse anyone. It's a bit like trying to get a handle on world politics. So here is a quick rundown to help you make up your mind.

**Hatha yoga** is the more traditional form and simpler than the others, so makes a good starting point. It teaches you the pranayama (breathing techniques), which are supposed to relax even the most stressed of us.

**Bikram** is a bit like trying to exercise in a sauna. The room is heated to 38–45 degrees Celsius, which makes the positions even more difficult and so gives you a more strenuous workout.

**Ashtanga** is the gold level of yogas. Beloved of celebrities such as Gwyneth, Madonna and Geri Halliwell, it is the most arduous form of yoga and consists of a series of linked postures that can take up to three hours to perform.

# RULES OF YOGIQUETTE

Like so many things in life, there are downsides to finding inner calm and gentle breathing. For a start, yoga studios can often be crammed mat to mat with stressed-out business types and competitive mothers desperate to achieve tranquillity and an uncreased face. Overstepping boundaries, ill feelings toward fellow yogis and strange noises are just some of the things you might find in the yoga class.

If you want to avoid a yoga bust up in the yoga studio, here are the top 10 do's and don'ts of yogiquette:

- **Don't** take up too much space with your mat. Yoga classes are often full to bursting, and there is nothing worse than someone who plonks themselves so near to you their arms are likely to thwack you in the face before you can say 'om'!
- **Do** arrive on time. Yoga may be about letting it be, but the teachers are sticklers for punctuality.
- **Don't** 'om' (the sound yogis make when they are performing their Asanas, or positions) at the top of your voice. After all, there is nothing worse than overenthusiastic yoga junkies taking over the class.
- **Do** try and keep awake during the Savasana (the resting pose at the end of class) – some people have been known to nod off and even snore.
- **Don't** start chatting about last night's must-see TV show with your neighbour. Yoga is not like the gym. Devotees take their holistic Vinyasas seriously, and that means silence.
- **Do** turn your mobile off. 21st century noise is exactly what you are supposed to be clearing in your head. Besides, if you have a really loud ringtone, you could send someone crashing down from their scorpion pose.
- **Don't** turn up with an expensive Gucci mat and a flash mat cover. Yoga is about being centred, not the centre of attention.
- **Do** make sure you're not showing more than you bargained for. Some positions, such as the downward dog, can cause 'spillage' so wearing proper fitting clothes will avoid any embarrassing moments.
- **Don't** break wind in class. This may seem strange, but yoga is designed to cleanse your mind and your body, and that means there can be violent expulsions of air during certain asanas. There is nothing more off-putting than a waft of last night's veggie burger just as you are getting to grips with a gravity-defying move.

- **Do** keep dodgy perspiration at bay. One of the big issues in yoga classes is the whiff of someone else's body odour, so spraying your pits with a fresh and fragrant anti-perspirant is only polite.

## TRANSFORM YOURSELF INTO A GYM BUNNY

None of us wants to hurtle towards smocks, comfy slacks and middle-age spread. One of the most convenient ways to get and stay fit is to join a gym. These shiny shrines to fitness were invented for people who would rather get the whole business of exercise done quickly and efficiently in a nice, bright room, with lots of friendly gym instructors and bouncy music, and without having to risk getting frostbite and sodden trainers from pounding the park in winter.

At the gym:

- You can run for hours and get sweaty on a treadmill even when it is only three degrees outside.
- You can exercise in front of a shiny plasma screen television and watch anything from the news to kick-arse pop music.
- You can read a newspaper or magazine, sip vitamin water and pedal a stationary bike all at the same time.
- You can make friends. Whether it is on the cross trainer or in the Zumba class, the gym widens your social circle, and you can chat and burn calories at the same time.
- There is always a gym instructor on tap to rev up your weights routine if you are getting bored doing lateral raises and lunges. If you want to become a buffed-up gym bunny, an instructor will also be only too happy to put you through your paces and create a fat-busting workout.
- You can while away a Friday night if you find yourself at a loose end. You will be surrounded by people who, like you, have nothing better to do than wor out and share a mango smoothie. Besides, most gyms have fancy health spa bars with comfy sofas, internet access and a great line in mung bean salad.

## A BRIEF GUIDE TO GYMIQUETTE

People do funny things in gyms. Suddenly, away from the normal codes of life, they throw caution to the wind and start running naked around the changing rooms or getting caught with their leotard down. Whilst it may not be the same as going to the opera or attending a formal dinner party, there are still rules when you go to a gym.

So for anyone who is unsure how to behave, here are some pointers:

### Eight things not to do in the gym

- **Don't** hog the water fountain by filling up your litre bottle. Take a few gulps and make way for the next person, and whatever you do, don't clamp your mouth round the nozzle!
- **Don't** let out a sudden grunt of exercise angst. Huffing and puffing in a lady-like fashion is fine, but leave the theatrics to the men.
- **Don't** leave puddles of sweat on the machines. Wipe and go.
- **Don't** leave your sodden towels on the machines, or worse, thick wads of sweaty gym tissue on the gym floor.
- **Don't** chat loudly on your mobile phone or have a humdinger of an argument whilst pounding the treadmill.
- **Don't** look like a disco diva when you are working out. Hot pink leotards, full-on makeup and acres of cleavage are simply unfair.
- **Don't** hog the mirrors. It is not a discothèque. Mirrored walls are there to monitor your progress and check you are doing the exercises properly. Preening and plucking your chin hairs is off-putting and high in yuck factor.
- **Don't** ogle the young cute guy in the slightly see-through cycling shorts. He will think you are attracted to him and either snort in derision – 'What's that middlie doing looking at me?' – or worse, will think he has caught himself a real-life cougar and put the moves on you.

## In the sauna

- **Don't** breathe loudly. Sounding like a freight train is not a pleasant sound for those wishing to relax. Imagine someone breathing hard in your ear while you're trying to enjoy yourself.
- **Do** wrap yourself in a towel. Just because some people enjoy the 'let it all hang out' sauna code isn't an excuse for full-on butt showing. It is a public place – for God's sake, cover up! Besides, would you like to sit in someone's naked sweat puddle?
- **Don't** talk loudly. Keep it to a low whisper if you must talk. Others in the sauna may not want to hear about the bad date you had last night.
- **Do** leave a polite space between you and your fellow saunee. Observe cinema rules – a space in between – and you should be okay.
- **Don't** try and make eye contact with your neighbour. Not even for a second. Especially if you have decided to flout the towel round the neither regions rule.

## In the changing room

- **Don't** parade up and down the changing rooms if you have a great bod. Other women will not be impressed by you showing them what they don't have.
- **Don't** ask to borrow another woman's deodorant or body lotion, even if you are late for a hot date and the shops are shut. It is embarrassing on so many levels. If she says yes because she's too polite, she will throw it away afterwards and resent you forever. If she says no, you will both experience a few seconds of toe-curling angst and she will still resent you.
- **Don't** plonk your rucksack, gym kit and sweaty trainers on the changing room benches. There is nothing worse than a gym diva who is having a 'this is my gym' moment and harrumphs loudly when fellow exercisers push her stuff out of the way.
- **Don't** strike up chatty, intimate conversations when you are butt naked. Be considerate and wrap a towel round yourself.
- **Don't** ever indulge in nude stretching!

## TOP CHAT-UP LINES MIDDLIES CAN USE IN THE GYM

A gym can be a hotbed of sexual tension. All those bottoms swathed in pink spandex or sweaty Lycra-clad bodies bobbing up and down on the spinning bikes. Not to mention the men who swim behind you to check out your wobbly bits. And then there is the lust potential of a his and hers steamy sauna. Really it is no surprise that gyms are reporting a surge in new members, all ready to meet their mate.

Whether you are single or in a relationship, there is nothing better for a middle-aged woman who thinks she has lost the 'phwoar' factor than to have a bit of a gym flirt.

Here are the top five chat up lines to break the ice:

- That's a great mp3 player. What are you listening to?
- Do you know who is the best personal trainer here? I really want to train for a marathon.
- Do you think that class/instructor is good?
- Can you teach me how to use this machine?
- Is that a barbell in your pants, or are you just pleased to see me?

## WHAT TO WEAR TO THE GYM

Slip on a fuchsia tank top, some black yoga leggings and a pair of Nike air trainers and you're all set. Not, as you might imagine, for a night out dancing, but for the gym. When you were younger it was okay to shuffle along in a pair of baggy grey trackie bottoms and an old washed out T-shirt and still manage to do the dishevelled rock chick look. Come the middlie years, we have to make a bit of an effort if we don't want to look like a scary bag lady as we heft weights and go red in the face. Looking good will help you feel more motivated and stick to your routine. That doesn't mean you have to wear figure-hugging Lycra to your first Zumba class. We all know the merits of the 'cover up.'

Here are the five basics that will give you a head start in the gym:

- Capri pants are the fashion-forward things to wear to the gym. The cropped just-over-the-knee leggings show the calf and makes the legs look longer.
- A vest with cutaway sleeves or a halterneck top will make your shoulders look broader and more sporty. Choose a sports top that has a built-in support bra to stop any sags and bags.
- A loose-fitting silky T-shirt will do wonders to hide any middle-aged spread, and worn over capri pants, will create a neat silhouette.
- Wear matching colours top and bottom if you want to slim down the sil-

houette. The all-in-one colour will draw attention away from any lumps and bumps.

- A fitting zip-up top is the perfect middlie coverall. It is like a safety blanket that you can sling on when it is chilly, or you are suddenly faced with a perfect gym babe. Alternatively tie it around your waist for butt cover up.

# GETTING FIT FROM NINE TO FIVE

If you work in an office, you are bound to spend a lot of time stuck at your desk in the seated position. Whilst you may get up to make the odd cup of coffee, pop out for a snack, or take a trip to the water cooler, researchers say that the majority of us who do desk bound jobs will spend 8-9 hours a day on our derrières. Which, come middle age, is a sure way to an expanding waistline and stress.

For the time-poor and workout-shy, there are ways to keep the body in top condition without spending hours on the Stairmaster.

## EIGHT TIPS TO GET FIT AT WORK

- Avoid the lift. Taking the stairs regularly will not only use up calories and kick-start your metabolism, it will tone your backside.
- Walk or cycle to work. If you take public transport, get off a few stops earlier and walk the rest of the journey.
- Go for a walk in your lunch break. Even looking in the shops or having a coffee at the café round the corner burns off calories and gets the muscles working.
- Never eat lunch at your desk. Even if the boss is glaring at you, get up, move around and get the circulation going.
- Drink plenty of water — like many places, offices can have dry air and feel more like the Sahara desert than a place of work.
- Keep away from the biscuit tray in the office kitchen. If you have to snack take some nuts, apples or rice cakes to work with you.
- Don't email colleagues if you can walk over and talk to them. Even getting up and down a few times a day will help you to keep in shape.
- If you're really energetic, start a running club with your workmates in the lunch hour. Include the boss, if you want to get promoted into the bargain — just don't outrun them at any cost.

# THE BINGO WING PLAN

Question: Why do middle-aged women wave from the wrist only, with their upper arms glued firmly to their sides?

Two words. Bingo wings.

It's terrible, isn't it? As if there wasn't enough to worry about when hitting the half-way point in our lives. Just as we are getting used to a few wrinkles, sags and bags, now we have to worry about that loose untoned flesh of the upper arm that seems to blight even the skinniest of women come middle age. In summer, sleeveless tops and those slippy dresses are banished from our wardrobes, as we reluctantly throw little cardis over our loose flesh.

## HOW TO BANISH BINGO WINGS

Whilst the sight of arm cellulite is enough to send any sane middlie into a tailspin, the good news is that anyone can get rid of them. Bingo wings are just fat, which means with the right diet and exercise you can tone them up. And even if you don't go to the gym or pay for a personal trainer you can banish 'arm cellulite' in the comfort of your own home.

First banish all sugar and those white carbs (white bread, pasta, rice) from your diet. Often that puckered flesh hanging off our arms like a strange alien is partly due to a bad diet. Try some good carbs like brown rice, lentils, chick peas and lots of protein to help promote strong Madonna-style muscle.

Next, you will need to do these exercises for at least 15 minutes every other day if you want to see a change.

**Triceps dips: 20 reps**
Grip either side of a chair seat behind you raise and lower yourself slowly up and down. This may feel as if you are undergoing some kind of torture, but persevere, it will get easier.

**Bicep curls: 20 reps**
For this you will need weights, or you can use a can of beans if you don't want to fork out on dumbbells. Holding the weights with your arms outstretched and downward, slowly lift them towards you, bending at the elbow.

# FAT BURNERS THAT HAVE NOTHING TO DO WITH THE GYM

For those of you who wouldn't be caught dead in an aerobics class or don't have the time for lengthy workouts in the gym, there are much easier ways to shed pounds and tone muscles without lifting weights. Scientists claim that daily activities such as walking the dog, gardening, or even fidgeting are guaranteed ways to shift pounds – and get this, they are free.

- **Walk the dog.** Taking your pooch (or a friend's) for a saunter round the park or in the countryside not only gets you fit, it helps you to slow down and clear your head of all those daily niggles.

- **Have sex.** There is nothing like some good old girl-on-boy action to get you hot, sweaty and fit into the bargain. Not only does it boost the immune system, release pent-up stress and make you feel happy and woozy (thanks to the release of endorphins) it helps you to maintain a close bond with your partner by the production of the intimacy boosting hormone, oxytocin. Cue post-coital snuggles and DVDs.

- **Garden.** All that deadheading, pruning, cutting and bending down to snip off the weeds are not only great stressbusters, but work up a sweat and strengthen muscles into the bargain. There is the added benefit of being in the fresh air and the feel-good factor of creating something.

- **Exercise at home.** Leaping up and down in your own living room to an exercise DVD is an easy and convenient way to keep fit. You can look as sweaty and scruffy as you like, lunge, grunt and do all sorts of anti-social things you couldn't get away with in the gym, and if you feel puffed or want a glug of something, you simply press pause and have a rest.

- **Fidget.** For those of you who are constantly jumping up to make a cuppa, or crossing and uncrossing your legs, you are in for a treat. A report by Professor James Levine at the Mayo Clinic in the US found that fidgeting can burn up to 350 calories a day. So start moving.

# THE HOUSEWORK BURN

Research suggests that our mothers burnt three times more calories than we do and they didn't have a yoga class in sight. Think of all those floors they scrubbed, the beds they flipped, the clothes they washed by hand and the fat-burning mangle. Yikes! Homemaking may have been a chore, but it certainly kept them fit. Nowadays, labour-saving devices, convenience foods and hours plonked in front of the TV have made the modern middlie sedentary and overweight.

**The 1950s housewife:**
- Spent three hours a day doing her housework.
- Washed clothes by hand.
- Wrung clothes through a mangle – great for the upper arms.
- Walked to the shops to buy groceries.
- Cooked fresh, homemade meals every day for the whole family.

**The noughties housewife:**
- Stuffs dirty clothes in the washing machine.
- Stuffs wet, clean clothes into the tumble dryer.
- Jumps in the car to do the weekly shop.
- Cooks pasta or a ready-cooked meal.
- Loads the dishwasher.
- Slumps in front of the telly and watches a good daytime soap.

## THE HOUSEWORK FITNESS PLAN

Did you know that housework can burn up to 100–200 calories an hour, which is pretty much the same as a light session of lifting weights? Turning your housework into a work-out is a win-win situation. Not only do you get a sparkling house and a happy hubby, but you are bound to firm up thighs and arms in the bargain.

Top tips for the 'housework burn':

- Get into the zone. Treat housework as an opportunity to get fit instead of a punishment.
- Before you start, put on some comfy, loose clothes so you can really move around.
- Put on one of your favourite records and turn up the volume – it will give you the added oomph to get sweeping and dusting.
- Use a wax polish instead of the usual spray cans. You will need to rub much harder to get a good shine and will tone the upper arms as you rub.
- Really stretch the upper body as you clean in the corners. It will give you a great workout.
- If you really want to burn calories, run up and down stairs as much as you can. Alternate rooms – for example, do the dusting downstairs then rush upstairs to do the bathroom, then vacuum the living room downstairs, and make the bed upstairs.
- Do the washing up by hand. Not only will you save money, you will work those upper arms again.
- Looking around your sparkling house after you've finished is an unbeatable boost, and you've saved all that money on the cleaner.

# 6.
# THE MIDLIFE FRIENDSHIP FORMULA
## BUSY, BUSY BEE

'Can do the 13th. Hmm, maybe not, think that Dad's birthday. How about the 21st or Saturday … if not, lets put a date for a catch-up in the diary for next month.'

Sound familiar?

Come midlife, we can find ourselves overstretched by work, family and other life stuff. Our schedules are too hectic to even have sex with our partner, let alone to block off an hour to meet a friend for coffee.

So is it any wonder that one of the first things to go as we hit middle age are our friendships? With fewer opportunities to hang out, even if we love them to bits, they are undernourished and kept afloat with apologetic emails and the odd Skype session.

Back in the golden age of friendship in our youth, we would spend whole afteroons and long evenings doing nothing much, just hanging out. Now we can just about fit in the 'guilt catch-up'. This is where you grab a quick skinny latte in your lunch hour with said friend who you haven't seen in ages. You chat a bit and then slope off; that guilty feeling has gone, and you can wait till the next time.

Yet are we making a mistake paying so little attention to our friendships? Studies consistently say that a good group of friends not only makes us happy, but helps relieve stress and gives us a sense of belonging.

And it's true – where would we be without a shoulder to cry on, someone to tell us that we are not going to die alone in a house full of cats, someone to hug us when we are lonely and tell us that we are not a mad old bat with a bottom the size of a medicine ball, or someone to tell us to hurry up and let's go and party.

In an ideal world, we would all have a super friend who is able to cover all the bases, yet in reality, most of us will have a handful of close friends who play different roles in our lives.

## THE FIVE FRIENDS YOU NEED

###  THE OLD FRIEND

You met at school or became best buddies at college. The point is, it doesn't really matter where you met. What matters is that they have known you for yonks. They were there when you came back from the hairdresser with the embarrassing poodle perm and pink leggings, they held your hair back when you got drunk on home made cider and threw up, and they know things about you, like how your mum drives you crazy, or the way your younger brother has really irritated you over the years. Not only that, they have witnessed your important milestones: your first boyfriend, first job, first breakup, and all the other life stuff that has made you what you are. The kind of back story you share naturally creates a bond and it means that you don't have to explain everything to each other. You just know.

## Pros of the old friend

- You can do that slobbing-out-together-in-jimjams-eating-taco-chips-and watching-trashy-movies thing, and feel really, really relaxed.
- You can cry in front of them.
- You can tease each other and you probably have pet names for each other.
- They instinctively know how you are feeling, and will put an arm round you without any prompting.

## THE COMPASSIONATE FRIEND

When we find a friend who is really compassionate, we cling onto them for dear life. They are the ones we phone up when we are having a bad day at the office, the children are ill, when we think our mum's having an affair – they always have the time to listen to us. For some reason, the CF has the capacity to absorb all our angst without feeling as if we have just dumped a whole load of emotional baggage in her lap. Broadminded and non-judgemental, she is the Mother Teresa of the friend world and worth her weight in gold.

## Pros of the CF

- They are like free therapy – and you get to drink during your sessions.
- Full of warmth and understanding, they are always there to offer support.
- They are like a mother substitute and will always invite you round for a good movie and some comfort food. They plump up your pillows, settle you in and make you feel as if you are five years old, safe and sound.

## THE FRIEND WHO LIVES ROUND THE CORNER

You huff and puff embarrassingly together through your weekly Zumba classes at the local gym, you spend hours nursing a cafe latte and gossiping about people in the neighbourhood, and she is probably the one you end up shopping with for the all-important LBD, because after all, she only lives two streets away. Your relationship with the FRC is based on the comfortable familiarity of seeing each other on a regular basis. She may not be the friend you turn to in a time of need, but she is the perfect 'polyfiller' to get you through a lonely Sunday afternoon or a Friday night alone.

### Pros of the FRC

- She invites you round for spaghetti carbonara when you have nothing in the fridge.
- You don't have to worry about getting drunk round at her place, as staggering down the street is easy peasy, even after two bottles of pinot grigio.
- She is the casual friend you bump into down the street, pop into the local wine bar with for 'just one spritzer,' and end up completely blotto with.

## THE GOOD TIME FRIEND – AKA THE SINGLE

She is always guaranteed to make you laugh, not because she tries to, but because she is naturally funny. Full of good humour and warmth, the GTF is like the human equivalent of popping a prozac. Even though her life may be a shambles – she's the one who has forgotten to have the child/get married/get a mortgage – she is the one who has always lived life on her terms, and you admire the way she is so resolutely herself.

### Pros of the GTF

- She is the one to phone when you are feeling bored or low.
- She knows all the best bars, restaurants and that private drinking club that is open after hours.
- She has an address book full of interesting men who, even if you are married, are just the tonic if you are having a bad boyfriend day or want a bit of attention.
- She has a wardrobe full of red satiny slutty numbers that she will always lend.
- She is the tart with the heart. Naughty but nice and with a heart of gold, your husband will hate her, but you love her verve and vitality.

## THE LEADER FRIEND

'Should I sell my flat in such a bad economy?' you ask. She will be the one with the stats and figures. 'Should I have an affair with the man from accounts?' She will tell you to get over it and work on your marriage. Eminently practical, unbelievably well-organised and not afraid to get down to the nitty gritty – in other words, everything you are not – she is the friend to turn to when you want some good old-fashioned advice. Frank and no-nonsense, the LF is the one who will tell you that miniskirts are for 15 year-olds and that it is time to get rid of the old whicker chairs round the dining table. Always the realist, they may come across as a bit hard sometimes, but they are essential to help us stay focused when we are in danger of making another irresponsible decision.

### Pros of the LF

- She is like a human RSJ, propping you up when you start to feel a bit wobbly or pathetic.
- She is the friend to draft in when the going gets tough. Never afraid to confront the difficult topics, she is the one who will tell it to you straight, whether you like it or not.
- She may not be the best friend to go to when you are teary, but she is the one who will ring you regularly with bits of useful information and numbers of 'people who can help'. Which is just her way of saying that she cares deeply.

## CAN YOU EVER BE FRIENDS WITH A MAN?

Ever since Billy Crystal said to Meg Ryan in the film *When Harry Met Sally*, 'Men and women can't be friends because the sex part always gets in the way', we have debated the cross-gender friendship with much zeal. Is it really out of the question to have a platonic friendship with a member of the opposite sex when you are in a loving relationship with another? And is the 'sex' factor always going to get in the way, even if you've never fancied him?

So he's great fun to be with, he makes you laugh and gives you a bloke's perspective on the world. You have long lunches together, go to the movies a deux and you once slept in the same hotel room (before present partner) and nothing happened.

From where you stand, it's just good fun, and seeing as he is so not your type, why on earth would your partner be jealous in the first place? The trouble is, no man wants to see their loved one being overly matey with another man. At best it will make him feel excluded, at worst he will be checking your mobile phone for 'sexting'!

If you do have a bloke as a friend, there are some ground rules:

- Always make sure you invite his girlfriend/wife when you go out.
- Don't spend ages on the phone during the evening. That is their time.
- Never call him up drunk and cry down the phone.
- Try to make friends with his partner. That way she will love you just as much as he does.
- If you start to feel an 'undercurrent' of attraction developing, get out – it is not worth the hassle.
- If you go out with his partner, don't start with the in jokes or stories about things you did together.

# THE FRIENDSHIP RULES

Even though life may be frantic a lot of the time, investing in our friendships is one of the most useful things we can do for ourselves.

### Rule one: Look at your own behaviour

The first step is to look at yourself and see how you behave in friendships. Are you the one always on hand with TLC (tender loving care) and a tub of her favourite Häagen-Dazs? Or maybe you are the one administering the home truths no one else dares to say. Or could you be the one everyone feels they should look after? It's important to understand your role in the relationships. Taking responsibility for the way you interact with someone and how it affects you is the first step to creating changes.

### Rule two: Don't hang on to a friendship that is beginning to feel like a drain.

Just because you both danced to Bananarama in the mid-80s doesn't mean you have to cling onto each other like limpets. As is often the case in midlife, people change and 20 years on we hardly recognise them. If you are still a bit of a hippie, like the cosy informality of spontaneous dinners and are still wearing last year's Ugg boots, and she is dressed 24/7 in Jil Sander suits and travels first class to places like Geneva, then there is the potential for a lot of tension. Not only will she look down on your student-like lifestyle and make you feel like a teenager, the idea of friendship is to make each other feel special, not like lifestyle freaks. Friendships can go past their sell-by date.

**Rule three: Don't over-whinge with friends**

That's the things about friends. We think, 'Look, they like me, so I can go on and on about the fact that my relationship is a disaster/my boss is a bully/the ins and outs of my mother's dementia are a drain.' Stop right there. Just because they are your friend does not mean you have to assault their earholes. There is always a sympathy cut-off point. I would say about two weeks. After that, you can mention the problem, but no crying and wailing please.

**Rule four: Don't be a friendship mug**

If you are the friend doing all the listening, all of the time, you might start to feel a bit put upon. We all know the friend who is so needy that they will bulldoze you with every problem, feeling and event of their lives. The trouble is, when something happens to you, they are miraculously out of reach. 'Sorry, got to go,' they say when they suspect you may need help. There should be mutual give and take and if you find yourself acting as her personal agony aunt, you need to distance yourself.

**Rule five: Don't do digi-friendship**

If you keep in touch only through email or text then it's not really a friendship any more. You need to make time and effort to keep a friendship alive, so if you think you really value this person, call them up and arrange to meet them for a coffee.

**Rule six: Don't impose your children on your friends**

If you have sulky toddlers and you are seeing a single friend or a friend with teenagers, then they may not take too kindly to temper tantrums and apple puree all over the new beige settee. Find out first if they mind if little Jemima and Johnny come round, and don't be angry if they don't want to be as involved in this area of your life. After all, do they really want to hear about your daughter's amazing drawings with crayon and paint and you wittering on about how your son is a baby Einstein?

## AVOID THE HAPPINESS VAMPIRES

We've all got them. These are the friends who never fail to make us feel bad, spread gossip and play mind games wherever they go – all the while pretending to be your best mate. They are the happiness vampires, and the quicker you get rid of them, the better you will feel. Have a look and see if you recognise any of these characters.

## The manipulator

She is the predator and you are fertile ground. This is how it starts.

She comes from nowhere and somehow appoints you her best friend. She invites you to parties, arranges playdates with her children and she dries your eyes when the hospital calls about your dad. Soon you get to rely on her so much you wonder what you did without someone as sweet as her.

Then one day she will stop calling. 'You haven't called for ages,' you say, panic in your voice.

'For God's sake,' she says, rolling her eyes, 'You're like my ex, don't you have a life?'

Bullseye! She has got you. She reeled you in, and just as you felt all cosy and comfy, she pulled the rug out from under your feet. At first you are gobsmacked, and then you start to feel hurt.

A few days later, just as you are feeling a bit better, she calls up out of the blue.

'I'm so sorry,' she wails, tears in her eyes. 'Don't you know you're my bestest friend?' Hugs and kisses. Phew, you think, she still likes me, and you are so happy to feel good again you accept her appology brunch and you are best chums. Until the next time.

She is the friend equivalent of the push and pull guy. In, out. In, out. She will do it again and again, until you finally wise up and walk away.

## The muck-raker

You're having a crisis. Your husband spends all his time out with the lads, or so he says, your children don't listen to you any more and you have an important deadline that's looming on the horizon.

As soon as the news is on the grapevine, this friend is always the first to invite you round for coffee. Trap set, she will pour you wine, dry your eyes and give you a shoulder to cry on. Thank God, you think, as you down another glass of her vintage chablis, someone to talk to, hiccup! Slightly squiffy, you blurt out all your problems and fears.

'Should I carry on taking the Prozac?' you confide for the first time to anyone.

'Do you think it was okay to cheat on the cooking test?' you bleat, as you get it all off your chest.

What you don't realise is that this friend is the worst person to confide in. Sure as eggs are eggs, she will be listening to you and plotting her next move. The muck-raker loves other people's misery. Most probably unhappy about her own life and insanely jealous of everyone else's, she delights in other people's disasters.

No sooner has she sqeezed every last morsel out of you, she will be on the phone at the club/gym spreading the dirt.

And if you manage to resurrect any slither of self worth back after she's finished with you, she will smile sweetly and deny the whole thing.

## The put-down merchant

'It's amazing, I've just landed a great new job and John and I are getting on like a house on fire.'

'Uh-huh. Great.' (pause) 'So are you working with Jacinta Powell?'

'Er, yes I am as a matter of fact.'

'Oh right-ho, hopefully you'll last longer than the rest of them.' (Put-down #1)

'What do you mean?' you say, scratching your forehead.

'Oh nothing,' she says and changes the subject.

'Guess what, I forgot to tell you, I saw your John the other day, at least I think it was him, kissing some woman on the cheeks – must have been his sister,' she says in a faux casual voice. (Put-down #2)

'Umm, he hasn't got a sister.'

'Oh silly me, always putting my foot in it,' she says gleefully, 'Anyway must hurry, have to go to that damn Hollywood party.' (Put-down #3)

A conversation with this friend is like tiptoeing through a minefield and finding yourself constantly stepping on bombs. By the time you've finished talking to her, your great job sounds like poo, your happy marriage feels as if it is breaking at the seams and all you want to do is crawl into bed and cry.

## The control freak

This one is the boss of everything. She makes all the decisions, she often wants to see you alone, and is always popping in whether you are busy or not.

She gets angry if you tell her you're busy, tired or going out with someone else, and thinks nothing of using all the tactics at her disposal to do things on her terms.

This friend is exhausting. She bellows down the phone at all hours. Dare to have a bar of chocolate, and she will be there telling you to eat goji berries before breakfast and exhorting you to go running three times a week with her. In short, you are her project and she thinks nothing of telling you how to live your life. She always wants to win every argument, and has set views on everything and everybody. Domineering, controlling and intolerant, she can reduce you to a quivering wreck unless you have the guts to stand up to her. Quite frankly, who has the time?

You know they are a toxic friend if ...

- You feel emotionally drained every time you see them. Good friends give as well as take.
- They always manage to say something that upsets you or makes you angry. Good friends don't play mental games with us.
- They talk about you behind your back. Good friends want the best for us.
- They flirt with your partner and try to take your other friends. Real friends never undermine our other relationships.
- They pretend to be your friend one minute and then pull the rug out from under your feet. Real friends are straightforward and we know where we stand with them.
- They dump all their problems on you, yet never listen to yours. Real friends are versed in the rules of give and take, and are engaged in your life and your problems.
- They lie to us and don't care. Real friends value honesty above all things.
- They put you down in front of others. Good friends support us by promoting our positive attributes.
- They ignore you when you are down. Good friends are there for us.

# WIN THE BATTLE

Since shooting them isn't an option, sometimes we have to learn how to deal with these difficult people so we don't end up in the madhouse.

## Set firm boundaries

Toxic people will often use you to further their own ends. They may use you as their sounding board whilst you listen helplessly, or they may put you down in public to feel better about themselves. It is important that you set firm boundaries as these will let them know what you are and aren't willing to put up with.

## Get over your guilt

Most toxic people are very skilled at making others feel guilty when they don't do what they want. This makes it particularly hard to set and maintain firm boundaries with them. But there is a way out of this dilemma: getting rid of your guilt. It is your own guilt that toxic people use to break down your boundaries.

## Do not defend yourself

When you avoid toxic people and you set boundaries with them, they frequently resort to accusing you, complaining and playing the victim in an attempt to get you to change your behaviour. One of the worst things you can do when this happens is to defend yourself. It is usually a futile action and it only keeps an immature dialogue going, which eventually helps the toxic person get what they want. You won't get anywhere with them by defending yourself and your actions.

And if all else fails, move to another country.

# Quiz

Try our quiz to find out what kind of friend you are.

**1 Your best friend is dating someone you hate. Do you:**
a) Say nothing; it is her life after all.
b) Say nothing but glare at him when she is not looking.
c) Tell her exactly what you think.

**2 Your friend is wearing a dress that is way too tight and short. Do you:**
a) Say nothing and hope someone else does.
b) Say nothing, but take her clothes shopping.
c) Tell her to grow up and get a longer skirt.

**3 How many close friends do you have?**
a) At least six.
b) A couple.
c) None, but I have a lot of acquaintances.

**4 Your friend is always late. What do you do?**
a) Say nothing and hope she changes her ways.
b) Say nothing at first, and then tell her jokingly to buy a watch.
c) Cut off all contact with her.

**5 How do you act around your friends?**
a) I make a lot of effort to please them as they are very important to me.
b) Relaxed and sometimes silly.
c) I tend to organise everyone around me.

**6 What do you think are the most important qualities in a friend?**
a) Loyalty and someone who is kind to me.
b) Like-mindedness and a sense of humour.
c) Someone who does what I say.

**7 You are getting ready for a party and a friend tells you you don't look good in the dress you are wearing. Do you?**
a) Change immediately. That is so embarrassing.
b) Ask her why. And if you agree, change.
c) Roll your eyes and let her know that you don't care what she thinks.

**Mostly A's:**
You seem to be a little bit anxious about standing up for what you believe in. A people pleaser, you think that if you disagree with your friends, you may lose them. You need to learn to value yourself as a good friend and develop more confidence.

**Mostly B's:**
You are a confident, outgoing person with close friends and lots of acquaintances. You like people, but you are not afraid to be yourself and stand up for who you are. This will stand you in good stead, and people will naturally gravitate towards you.

**Mostly C's:**
You are a bit absorbed in yourself, and find it difficult to empathise with how other people are feeling. Maybe it is time to let people in and reveal a bit of your vulnerability. You will find that when you accept yourself, you will naturally be able to accept other people for who they are.

# 7.
# NOT TONIGHT DARLING
## THE MIDLIFE MARRIAGE

# HOW TO GET THE MARRIAGE BACK ON ITS FEET

You wake up one morning and look across the kitchen table. There he is, the man you fell in love with. He is making loud slurping noises as he gulps down his tea and scraping the burnt bits off his toast straight onto the kitchen table. As you wipe up the mess, you are gripped by a terrible thought.

'Is this it?' you think, as he scratches his nether regions and gives a loud resounding burp. Am I going to have to put up with this for the next 30-odd years?

What was once an exciting, loving relationship has now morphed into a medley of daily bickering, dinners eaten in silence and the odd night of sleeping on the couch.

And the pressures of midlife don't help. Running a home, bringing up children and coping with the day-to-day domestic routine can wear us down. The fact is, as a lot of people reach their 40s, they can't paper over the cracks any more. Whether your romantic life has taken a plunge, or you have simply grown apart, suddenly it's no longer fun.

The truth is, scratch the surface of a lot of happy couples, and there is bound to be a sliding scale of irritations and resentments that have built up over the years.

Here are five signs that the relationship is in need of the some TLC:

- He forgets your birthday, even though you've put it in the calendar and circled it in red!
- Your partner/you are watching internet porn regularly.
- You make him his favourite meal and he just grunts and eats it in front of the football.
- You tell him what irritates you and he carries on doing the same thing.
- Sex is just another chore on your list of things to do.

## GET A RELATIONSHIP TUNE-UP

Chances are, all you need is to re-establish the closeness that has been lost with all life's 'stuff' getting in the way. The good news is that many of the so-called problems are common to a lot of couples, and there are simple and effective techniques that can help. So in order to start enjoying life together again, book in a relationship tune-up.

- Make a list of all the things you want to change in the relationship and ask him to do the same. Be reasonable. Munching salad too loudly or leaving the loo seat up may be irritating, but it is hardly the stuff of divorce. It is better to concentrate on slightly more serious areas. Maybe you want more support around the house, maybe he feels you don't show him enough approval. Communicating these needs to each other is the first step in reaching a compromise.

- Make sure you listen to what he says and vice versa. A good technique is to get him to repeat what you have said back to you. It makes you both really have to listen and think about it. You'll be surprised how much you start to learn about each other once you make your feelings and needs heard.

- Don't play the blame game. It is easy for a conversation to descend into a power struggle once one of you starts pointing the finger. The aim is to respect what each other says, so that you can salvage your relationship, not to win the argument and do a victory dance! Keep your statements brief and to the point. Avoid saying things like, 'the trouble with you is,' or 'if only you'. Instead say things like, 'in order for us to be closer' or 'I need you to'.

- If you find it difficult to avoid getting personal, try the roses and bricks approach. For example, start by saying, 'Whilst I appreciate you're busy, I feel really lonely and neglected when you spend all night out with your mates.' This way you are showing that you understand his feelings whilst asserting your own needs.

- Discuss where each of you sees areas for improvement, and give solutions. For example, if you want to throttle him every time you see his wet towel thrown on the bathroom floor, tell him how it makes you feel and offer to buy a washing basket.

- Make time to talk to each other. Even if you are both rushing around doing things, there is always time for a coffee, Sunday lunch, or just making each other breakfast and reading the newspapers in bed. It is the first step to making an effort for the sake of the relationship.

- Keep it brief. Men respond to facts, not emotional outbursts. You may feel hurt and resentful about how he never puts the trash out or never bothers to phone if he is going to be late, but resist the urge to regurgitate all his past misdemeanours. State the problem: 'When you don't call, it makes me worry. I would appreciate it if you could think of my feelings next time.' And then walk off and do something else.

## HOW TO DEAL WITH THE DOMESTIC STAND OFF

Does he refuse to pick up his dirty socks? Do you become snippy if he leaves the dishes unwashed?

Why is it that getting men to do the household chores can seem as difficult as climbing Kilimanjaro in flip-flops?

According to psychologists, activities such as the washing up or ironing are perceived as a woman's role (as if we didn't know that already), and just the sight of a pair of rubber gloves can have him running to the local bar faster than you can say, 'Put on the apron.' If his idea of fairness is you doing 75 per cent of the chores, then consider the following:

- Suggest you plan a roster and stick it on the wall. Mark out precise chores that each of you have to do, and make sure you stick to it.
- Maybe he could do some of the more 'manly' activities – taking rubbish or recycling out for example – and you could offer to do the dishes.
- Don't nag him. Men hate to be told what to do. If you say, 'do the washing up,' chances are he will dig his heels in and watch the telly.
- On the other hand, if you make a suggestion of what needs doing, he might do it more willingly. And if he does get his butt off the sofa, don't hover over him like his mother.
- Make it fun. Offer to cook the dinner in a bikini (when you're alone) if he will clear up afterwards.
- According to scientists, spraying the air with a citrus scent may help to get his domestic juices going. Apparently the smell can subliminally influence your partner's thoughts and make him think of cleaning products!

# THE INCREDIBLE SULK

What to do if your partner gives you the silent treatment?

Why do men sulk? There you are having an argument about something quite trivial. You will air your grievances, state your case and clear the air. The sulker, on the other hand, has only just begun. Unable to let rip with a few chosen expletives, he would rather slump on the sofa and ignore you. The thing is, 30 minutes later, you have forgotten all about the argument and are ready to get on with the day in a friendly fashion. The sulker, on the other hand, is now well into the first phase of his sulkathon. 'Cup of tea, darling?' you say, in an effort to diffuse the ticking male time bomb you see before you. He says nothing, and continues staring out of the window. That is the trouble with sulkers – they can go on for hours or days, punishing you and poisoning the atmosphere like radon gas. And the longer it goes on, the more resentful they feel. They sit wallowing in their injured pride and nursing their supposed grievances like a spoilt child.

So what can you do if you find yourself on the receiving end of a full-on sulk?

- As tempting as it is, don't counter-sulk. It will set up a power struggle and he will feel even more justified in his behaviour. Be prepared for the long haul if you do decide to volley back some sulk tactics of your own – remember, though, they are pros at this kind of behaviour.
- Make one conciliatory gesture to show good will. If he walks/turns away, then leave it. Any more attempts will only make you look desperate for his attention and he will pay you back with even more sulking. Sulking is about power and punishment. Don't be a willing victim.
- The answer is to get on with your life as if nothing was wrong, and wait for him to come out from under his stone. Go out for the day with friends, or even better, book yourself into a hotel and come back the following day. You are letting him know that you don't need or want to put up with his behaviour and have other options. Besides, without anyone to punish, they will soon get bored and want your attention again.

# HOW TO GET ON WITH THE MOTHER-IN-LAW

She may seem like a battleaxe and she may treat you as if you are a speck of dust on the floor, but she's his mum and he loves her. So come on, she's got to have some good points!

- Ask for her advice: maybe she is lonely and wants to feel needed.
- Find out what she is good at, and the next time she comes round, ask her how to prepare a certain dish, or about something you know she prides herself on her expertise in. It will make her feel more involved and she may soften towards you
- Take her shopping. It shows that you are thinking of her. There is nothing like a bit of retail therapy to get the bonding going. Treat her to coffee and cake afterwards and if things have gone well, you may even start to get on.
- No matter how many times she criticises your cooking, your child-rearing skills or the fact that there is a layer of dust on the TV, don't have a shouting match. If you do, your partner will have to take sides, and he will resent you for putting him in a difficult position. If she really is unbearable, explain to your partner how you feel and suggest he spends some quality time with her alone.
- If she is the type to make little jibes at you, resist the urge to throw your glass of wine over her. Instead, laugh it off with a counter-joke. Her: 'Oh, that's a lovely dress dear, my cleaner has one just like it.' You: 'Yes, your son bought me this dress. He got it from a charity shop.' Subtext: You are telling her that you won't stand for her snide comments. By making a joke, you are keeping the peace.

# HOW TO BE A MIDLIFE ROMANTIC

Are you kidding? Romance? I've got the dinner to make, the kids to bathe, the dogs to walk, he'll be lucky if he gets a quick cuddle before lights out at 10.30. Sound familiar? In today's fast-paced life, is it any surprise that, come midlife, we are all too exhausted to speak to our other half, let alone make love in the moonlight?

If your relationship is beginning to feel as flat as a collapsed soufflé, then why not try the following:

- Mix things up a bit. The thing about long relationships is that things can become predictable. Over the years practicalities have taken the place of romance and instead of chats on the beach, it's more a case of, 'Did you buy the bin liners, dear, because we've run out.' Take a break from the mundane and start doing new things. Book a weekend away at a hotel and spa with a double massage session. Sharing moments with a loved one will bring you closer together and reignite those feelings that have been dampened through decades of domestic routine.

- Go for a walk in a forest/the mountains/along a windswept beach. Spending time out in the wilds will not only heighten your senses, but having a challenging goal like finishing a long walk or climbing a mountain will make you feel more connected.

- Turn off the TV and start talking. One of the death knells for any relationship is to spend hours staring at the screen. Watching scripted dramas about other people's lives, whilst you are zoned out with a pack of crisps and a drink by your side, is a quick route to relationship apathy.

- Have shared activities. Join a tennis club, start your own 'games night' or learn a language together. Having shared goals will bring you closer together.

- Send funny/sexy/romantic texts to each other. Surprise each other with little gifts every now and then. Knowing that someone is thinking about us really gives us a lift and puts a bit of magic into our day.

- Give him a hug or a kiss for no reason. Maintaining affectionate touch is one of the things that gets lost when we become more like flatmates than a couple.

# BEWARE OF WHAT YOU SHARE

In the courtship days it was easy to keep a sense of mystery about ourselves. Yet the longer you are together, the harder it is to keep that mystique alive. So why is it that in today's let-it-all-hang-out society, so many couples believe in the 'we share everything' mantra. Whether it's talking about hot flushes and cramps or flossing whilst he's flushing, somehow if you are not privy to each other's personal habits, then you are not really bonding.

Helloooo!

If you want to keep the flame alive, then hold back on the details.

**What not to share:**

- Don't, whatever you do, show him your big pants. If you are wearing a bit of control underwear, he doesn't need to see it. After all, the point of Spanx is to create the illusion of a lump-free silhouette. Don't ruin the picture by revealing your oversized gym knickers and all your tricks.
- Don't divulge your grooming habits. Waxing, shaving, flossing, tweezing chin hairs and all those other girlie grooming routines should be done behind closed doors. After all, he doesn't need to know that you wax your moustache or how your legs are always as smooth as a baby's bottom. Maintaining a bit of feminine mystique, especially in long-term relationships, goes a long way to keeping the romance alive.
- Don't share the bathroom. You may be pressed for time and doubling up in the bathroom may seem like a good idea, but cleaning your teeth while he's doing his ablutions could scar you for life. Keep the bathroom door locked or better still, have separate bathrooms.
- Don't confide too much. If you want to have a good old whinge about the dreaded inner thigh cellulite or the state of your bingo wings, it's often better to phone a friend. Chances are he hasn't ever thought about your wobbly bits, so why alert him to them now?

# NOT TONIGHT DARLING

**How to spice up your sex life**

It is a Saturday night and you're both tired. You've prepared the dinner, loaded the dishwasher and sorted out the dirty laundry. By the time you get to bed you are exhausted.

A quick romp – you must be joking!

You can just about muster a half-hearted peck on the cheek and a cuddle, and then it's lights out at 10.30, eyemask on and earplugs in. It is a sad fact of life, but as we get older many couples get so bogged down in the humdrum minutiae of tidying up, supermarkets and child rearing, that our sex lives can go a bit limp. Factor in lack of sleep, busy schedules and long working hours and soon the only thing with any spark left in it is the plug.

Truth is, after years of marriage we are unlikely to jump into bed with the same gusto as we did in the honeymoon period. After a while, we may all need to make a bit of an effort when it comes to getting some good old horizontal hoopla!

If you want to up the ante, try some of these suggestions:

- Wear sexy underwear around the house. Buy something different to your usual style. Don't hold back on the 'naughty' factor. Give him an eyeful when he is watching the telly (not during sport – or else you will have stiff competition for his attention) and watch him get hot under the collar. Men are visual creatures so if you parade about in your pink lacy number, he will appreciate it.
- Look good around the house. If your usual knocking-around clothes consist of a pair of old jimjams with designs of bunny rabbits on them, shame on you! Invest in some lovely lounge pants (basically tracksuit/yoga bottoms made out of posh material) and a soft cotton top. Wearing fabrics that are nice to the touch will make you feel yummy and comfortable, and he will be desperate to get his hands on you.
- If you want to get into a romantic mood, but you have spent the last hour stuck in a traffic jam or queuing at the supermarket, you will need to unwind first. Light some aromatherapy candles and run a warm, sensual bath. Sprinkle a few drops of lavender, sandalwood or patchouli oil on the water to give it a lovely smell. Now lie back and luxuriate. When you feel rested, run your partner a similar bath and you can prepare yourself in the bedroom.
- Get a good bed. There is nothing worse than a lumpy old mattress with a coffee-stained duvet to dampen sexual desire. Invest in a new bouncy mattress and a thick cotton duvet cover. Spray jasmine scent over the bed to create a fresh spring like feel.
- Get a goodie box. Sex toys, from a rampant rabbit to furry handcuffs and fruit lubes, are fun. They can help to loosen up any inhibitions and will give you instant va va voom in the bedroom. By using some props you and your partner will discover new things about each other and soon you will be ravishing

each other under the sheets instead of being glued to the TV.

- Don't give your 'parts' pet names. Really, calling him 'Captain Happy' would be enough to make anything droop.
- If you always take your love to the bedroom, it is time to relocate. Try having some fun on the kitchen table, or take it to the laundry room; there is nothing like a vibrating washing machine for some added jig appeal. Surprise him in the living room wearing a negligee and stockings. Put some music on and give him a few moves. He will think it is his birthday and Christmas all rolled into one.
- Take a shower together and make use of beautiful smelling oils to awaken the senses.
- Take your love trysts out into the garden (in summer only!). The smell of the grass and the flowers will add extra sensory appeal, and there is nothing like being taken against the shed wall to liven up your sex life. It may be wise to wait till dusk – you don't want the neighbours peering over the fence.
- Get a room in an expensive hotel – anything cheap and that is what you'll feel. Being away from your familiar surroundings and your usual life can do wonders to reignite the flames of passion. Go the full nine yards and order a bottle of chilled wine/champagne and strawberries and enjoy the decadence of it all.
- Chat him up: arrange to meet him in a downtown bar and surprise him as someone else. Sometimes role playing is a great way to create distance and bring back that heady feeling you had at the beginning of a relationship. Dress up in stockings and a silk skirt and let him fantasise.

# DANGEROUS LIAISONS: THE MIDLIFE AFFAIR

So what happens if you are stuck in a so-so marriage that is lacking any spark, but isn't bad enough to leave? Generations ago, we would have been content with a wink from the postman and some sponge cake laced with gin. Today's melancholy midlifer is more likely to reach for the Prozac and some forbidden TLC (tender loving care) in the arms of a lover. Whether it is a clinch in the stationery cupboard with a fellow worker, an illicit grope at a party or a full-on love tryst, today's 40-something woman is getting her adventure where she can.

## SIX REASONS TO HAVE AN AFFAIR

- Your emotional needs are not being met.
- You are in a sexless marriage, but you don't want to leave.
- Your partner takes you for granted. You want to feel desired again.
- He has had an affair.
- You are sexually bored. You have your partner's moves down pat.
- You want some fun before you become a wrinkled old prune.

## HOW TO BE A LOVE RAT AND GET AWAY WITH IT

It is unlikely that you will wake up one morning and think, 'You know what? It's Friday, I think I'll have an affair.' It is more likely to be something that has been building up inside you for a while. There may be vague feelings of boredom, bedroom fatigue or a sudden desire to feel young and attractive again. Simply put, there comes a point where you may get fed up with the avalanche of ironing, the school run, and the potbellied husband slobbed out on the sofa waiting for his dinner.

After all, affairs happen. You get a wink from your handsome neighbour, you start flirting with Paul in the art department or a chance encounter on a train turns out to be more than just a pleasant chat. Suddenly you are 'sexting' like mad, lying awake at night dreaming of his touch. You get fit, buy new clothes and for the first time in years, you feel alive!

## WHAT'S NOT TO LIKE?

Being found out, that's what!

Imagine the scenario: Someone spots you in that out-of-the-way little bistro and texts your partner an incriminating photo; your partner reads one of your emails or you forget to hide the credit card bill; the next minute – bam!

The rage is his, the guilt is yours, and the years of trust and respect are torn apart in one moment. And then the divorce papers land in your lap. Job done. Marriage over.

An affair has got to be one of the most risky things anyone can do to a relationship. That's what stops the majority of us replying to the handsome neighbour's text or giving our telephone number to the man on the train.

So, if you are just about to enter a hotel room with your boss, ask yourself if you have the stomach for all the lies, deceit and the fear of being found out. If you set the infidelity ball rolling and find yourself racked with guilt, unable to sleep, desperate to tap your husband on the shoulder and confess the whole sordid business, then you are better off reading some steamy mummy porn and having a scented bubble bath. If, on the other hand, the thought of having the accounts manager on the meeting desk is just soooo enticing, then read on.

## PREPARATION IS KEY

- Organise, organise, organise – one slip-up could mean the end of your relationship. Don't meet him in your area. Another town is definitely advisable. And resist the urge to go to popular places; chances are someone you know will be there too.

- Don't behave out of the ordinary at home. If you start singing *Love Is In The Air* and dancing like a nutter, then your partner will either think you're going loopy or something is up. Sometimes women either become more intolerant of their partners when they are having an affair, or they feel so guilty they leave little mints on their pillow and make their favourite meals every day! For God's sake, act normal.

- Don't be sloppy: stands to reason. But why is it that some men and women who are having a bit on the side don't think it would be wise to delete all those incriminating texts and phone numbers. Don't get me started about leaving itemised phone bills around the house. Do not underestimate the suspicious partner who scrolls through your Blackberry when you are in the shower, or dials every number on the bill they don't recognise, from your phone!

- Be on the same page as your lover: don't have a roll in the hay with a single man looking to get married, as you could have a male bunny boiler on your hands. You both need to have a similar goal. If you do hook up with the personal trainer, you are both probably just in it for the sex. But make sure he doesn't see you as more than a wonderful diversion from everyday life.
- Don't stay in it too long. Unless you fall in love and marry your lover, you should probably put a time limit on the affair, a year tops, if you don't want things to get too complicated. After all, you are in for the excitement it brings to your life, not to cause a marital World War 3.

## FOUR WAY TO TELL IF HE IS HAVING AN AFFAIR

Here are the signs:

- He suddenly starts looking incredibly smart. When your jeans-and-sweat-shirt-wearing partner morphs into a smart-shirt-and-chinos guy, it is time to get a little bit suspicious.
- They get passionate about new things. If your husband is an occasional listener of pop music and he suddenly starts talking about the joys of Beethoven's Fifth and Eric Clapton's riffs, then something is going on.
- You start getting more and different sex. It is not always the case that a man having an affair will suddenly claim to have a headache when it comes to activity between the sheets. Often they are so turned on by their new lover that they want more sex – that, or they are feeling very, very guilty.
- They hide the mobile or rush to answer it. If your man usually leaves his mobile lying around the house and suddenly it is always in his pocket/hand, then he is hiding something.

Of course, these signs might have nothing to do with anything. Your partner could just be going mad. Trust your intuition and be more vigilant, but don't accuse until you have proof!

# HOW TO BREAK UP WITHOUT CRACKING UP

We all know that relationships can be hard work, and that with a bit of tweaking we can iron out some of the emotional glitches. But what if a relationship is all hard work? What about if you feel miserable most of the time?

Then what?

## SEVEN SIGNS THAT A MARRIAGE IS ON THE ROCKS

- I have a growing suspicion that I am married to a sociopath.
- I don't think we have the same core values.
- He has copped off with his secretary.
- The thought of going home at night gives me an attack of the heebie-jeebies.
- I have been trying to improve things for years and nothing works.
- He is a bully.
- I absolutely do not want to grow old with him.

## HOW TO MAKE A CLEAN EXIT

Leaving someone we have loved, spent a large part of our lives with and possibly had children with, is never going to be easy. Indeed it is bound to be one of the most painful things we can go through, and comes with a whole lorryload of grief and anger. However, if you have tried to repair the damage and you have failed, then it is better to cut your losses than stay in a loveless marriage that is grinding you both down.

**Here are some suggestions:**

- Avoid doing the break-up talk in a public restaurant. Contrary to popular belief, the fear of causing a scene will not stop him pouring his double martini over you.
- Ditto breaking up halfway through the summer holiday because you have finally had enough. This just means you either take the next flight home (at extra cost to you) or you will have to suffer another week of 24-hour sulking.
- Plan when you are going to leave. Mark out a quiet time at home and keep calm. If you are exiting a marriage, then it is going to take a long time and you will need to maintain a working friendship if you don't want to end up a nervous wreck.

- Have emotional manners. Don't list all the things you hate about him. After all, you are leaving, so you don't need to win the argument as well. Things like, 'It is better this way for both of us, this way we can get on with our lives' are corny but may avoid tears and tantrums.
- Be kind. Let him have the Elvis CD and the *Mad Men* box set – they are only things after all. Think how good you will feel if you manage to act like the mature one.

# 8.

# THE SINGLES FILE
## THE MIDLIFE DATING PLAN

# RISE OF THE MIDLIFE SINGLETON

There's nothing wrong with being single in midlife. Yeah, right, I can hear you say. No man to watch reruns of *Hawaii Five O* with, give you a cuddle when you've had a tough day at work, or simply scoop you up in his arms and make you feel you are the most important thing in his life. And it is true, being in a loving, supportive relationship where you both have the same taste in films, finish each others sentences and still feel he is the yin to your yang, is the best of all possible worlds. But come midlife, things don't always work out as we hoped. For whatever reasons, you may find yourself suddenly alone.

**You may be single because:**
- You've stormed out on your partner/husband.
- He's left you because you are the wrong one/he's found someone else.
- You both agree the relationship has run its course.
- You have never wed and bred, and are still looking for Mr Soul Mate.
- Your partner/husband has passed away.
- You picked the wrong man.

So here you are alone, staring out of the window wondering where it all went wrong. If only I had been quieter/sweeter/not complained so much maybe, just maybe ...

Stop right there.

The truth of the matter is, sometimes relationships go wrong. We change, we want different things and for whatever reason, the love ends. You squabble over the CD collection sell the 50-inch plasma screen telly and then you nurse your lonely heart.

Before you start thinking there is something radically wrong with you, nowadays there are more middle-aged singletons than ever before. More and more women are either delaying marriage in the search for Mr Right or are over their first marriage by the time they hit their 40s. So don't feel bad that your relationship didn't make it. Endings are never easy or fun and often include a lot of pain.

At this point, you need to lick your wounds. Often the first months after ending a relationship are the most difficult. The emotions that kick in can be devastating and painful especially if it is a divorce. You need to go through the process before you can move on Everyone is different, but at some point, you will feel yourself coming out of the 'dump tunnel.

Here are some do's and don'ts:

- **Do** stay at home. This is the time to recuperate. Stay indoors, watch upbeat movies, read and invite over close female friends (men are useless unless they are gay) loaded with wine, chocolates and lots of TLC. You can shout, scream and and call him all the names under the sun and they will be on your side.
- **Don't** ring, email or text him. It may be tempting to hear his familiar voice and 'discuss the breakup/divorce'. But believe me, it will only bring back painful memories and you will compromise your recovery. A clean break – unless there are children, and then you should keep it purely practical – is the best way to get over him.
- **Do** whine, cry or complain over the phone to your friends, sisters or chums for a few weeks or months only. We all need to get the emotions out of our system. If you carry on too long though, they may get weary, stage an intervention and cut you off cold turkey.
- **Don't** go into dump denial. It's only natural to feel hate, resentment or anger towards him. If you don't work through your feelings, you will never feel the relief and sheer joy of coming through the other side.

## THE POWER OF ONE

After you've shouted, punched the pillow and cried for what seems like ages, you may actually start to enjoy being alone. The first thing you  should know is that there are a lot of advantages to being single.

Being single means:

- You have ultimate control of the television remote, the stereo, and whether you want to lie in a silent room or have the radio blaring out pop tunes.
- You get to go to bed as early or late as you like without a grumpy male switching the light on and talking loudly in your ear.
- You get to set the alarm.
- You can lie in till noon, drink a cappuccino in bed and read the papers.
- You can leave a party after the first drink or just before dawn.
- You can spend all your money on new clothes and extravagantly-priced shoes without having to explain it to anyone.
- You can buy a pink leopard-skin throw for the sofa and no one will mind.

- You can eat what you want, whether it is brown rice and tofu or mozzarella and martinis – the choice is yours.
- You don't have to compromise. Ever!
- Your life is like an episode of *Sex and the City*. Only you're older, poorer and probably don't have a wardrobe full of Manolo slingbacks.
- Every time you go to dinner, the opera or a walk with friends, you think you might meet 'the one'!
- You can wander through the galleries on a Sunday afternoon and meet friends for dinner without having to worry about all those pre-Monday chores like sewing on name tags for the children or cooking the family supper.
- You don't have to pretend you love rock-climbing or skiing just because he does.
- You can have long Sunday lunches with your old friends and you will never have to put up with him glaring at you when he gets bored after half an hour.
- You can get the creative juices going. Try an art class, learn how to sail or basket weave, the choice is yours.

## THE JOYS OF LIVING ALONE

Instead of worrying about dying alone and being eaten by your Alsatians, à la Bridget Jones, why not discover the freedoms of living on your own without the clutter and noise of a man?

- You can start to live by your own rules.
- There is no man messing up your bathroom, bedroom or living room with grubby underpants and half-eaten pizza.
- You can play Status Quo or listen to the radio whilst you make the coffee in the morning, without him breathing over your shoulder and switching channels.
- You can paint your kitchen blue, your bathroom bright yellow and hang fairy lights over the bed without getting the go-ahead from him.
- You can lock the door behind you, make youself a wonderful meal, pour yourself a glass of wine and watch one of those romantic comedies without him chattering in your ear because he is bored.
- You can clip your toenails, shave your legs and do all that secret single behaviour that men don't realise exists.

- Think of all the shut-eye you can catch up on, now that you don't have him snoring next to you. You can snuggle up in your duvet and know that for eight hours there will be no duvet war, noisy toilet trips and the alarm bell ringing in your ears at 6 a.m.
- Your fridge will be stocked full of healthy treats, alfalfa seeds and a bottle of vodka just in case. What it won't have is last week's Indian curry complete with a layer of mould, bottles of beer and a super pack of economy sausages.
- Your bathroom will be spotless. There will no rancid towels stuffed in the laundry basket creating a strange pong around the flat, no trail of toothpaste round the sink or black tide marks left around the bath. He's gone and so has all his blokey bathroom behaviour.

## WHAT YOUR FRIENDS THINK OF YOU

Whilst you may be enjoying your freewheeling lifestyle, other people may not be celebrating your single status. A lot of married women, including your friends, will now be wary of you. For a start, you are out of synch with everyone else. Not only will you be mucking up the seating plans at dinner parties, you're a square peg in round 'couply' holes.

They're talking the merits of family holidays, you're talking hot men you spotted on the subway and the joys of lying in bed on a Sunday morning. More importantly, you have now become a threat to the status quo. Well, you're single aren't you, which makes you a) desperate for sex and b) desperate for sex with their men. That is how some of them will see it anyway.

Once you break up or divorce, be prepared to be sent to social Siberia. The invites to dinner will dry up like the Gobi desert, mouths will drop as you walk in the room, and there will be an uncomfortable shuffling of feet as they usher their potbellied husbands out the door.

Worse still, what happens when one of these codgers decides to make a pass at you? Again you're single, so you must be desperate and up for it. This can often happen at a wedding, party or even at the pub. They will:

- Play footsie with you under the table.
- Grope your bottom on the dance floor at weddings.
- Look so far down your cleavage you will be honour-bound to ask if they need a snorkel.
- Get you in a corner and start telling you how their wife doesn't understand

them, just as their podgy hand clamps itself around your upper thigh.
- Phone you up and ask if you want a coffee.
- Cop a feel the moment you are alone in the kitchen or going to the washroom.
- Say things like, 'So when was the last time, you… you know what! Eh, fancy a quick one?'

And if you ever dare to complain, they will harrumph, deny everything and turn bright red. Their wives will think that it is you who egged them on, and then not only will you be single, you will be seen as a husband stealer. The best thing is to say nothing, leave them to their unhappy marriages and hang out with your good friends.

# THE MIDLIFE DATING PLAN

Okay, so once you are finally comfortable with being on your own, you have managed to fend off your neighbour's randy husband, and you have a supportive girl gang, you are ready to date again.

A word of caution: It would be naïve to think that there are not going to be challenges in finding a new loved one in midlife. You haven't dated for yonks, you have spent the last decade in cosy companionship and comfy clothes and don't get me started on what to wear on a first date. Yikes! It is easy to feel a bit daunted and start to panic.

When you start to date in midlife, you don't know what to expect. It all seems so daunting. After all, the last time you sat batting your eyelids at some random guy at a party was circa 1988, and you were wearing leopard-skin leggings, a sparkly T-shirt and drinking warm cider. In midlife, things are a bit different.

## KNOW WHAT YOU WANT

Before you start dating, try to figure out what you want from a relationship. Think about your expectations. Maybe after years of a serious relationship or marriage, dating for fun with no strings attached could be just what you need to get you back on track. But if there is an expectation of a serious relationship, then it is best to seek out someone who is looking for the same thing.

So how do you know if you are ready to commit again, or if you are still in the 'shopping around' phase?

You're in it for the short-term if:

- You are having so much fun being modern and single.
- You are still licking your wounds and you want to shop around.
- You just want some fun company for now.
- This is a sex stopgap to keep you looking and feeling desirable.

You're in it for the long-term if:

- You feel lonely watching box-sets and going to bed at nine on your own.
- You find yourself watching romantic old movies and wishing you were the heroine.
- You are ready to give your heart again.
- You are tired of being the third wheel at parties and dinners and want to be part of a couple again.

# INTERNET DATING

Chances are when you were single, you were still dating in the traditional way – meeting someone at a party, a bar or through friends. Nowadays things have changed. For a start, online dating has lost all its lonely hearts stigma, and is now just another way to find love or companionship.

## Pros

- Joining internet dating sites is perfect for the busy midlifer who hasn't got time to spend her evenings out in bars.
- There is so much choice out there. You can join an 'older dating', 'matchmaking' or even 'executive' site, or all three.
- You can fire off warm, funny messages when you are in bed with your hair in curlers and he won't be any the wiser.
- It is much easier to handle rejection. If you don't get a reply from some guy online, who cares? Move on and talk to someone new. Far better than an awkward pause in a bar during which the man of your dreams rushes off to talk to the wall.
- It may not have the same romantic touch as eyes meeting across a crowded room, but for efficiency and time saving it scores a 10.

**Cons:**

- The chances of him being a nutter are infinitely greater.
- Who doesn't present a better version of themselves on the internet? When he says 'middle-aged', he is probably in his dotage with false teeth.
- 'Portly' probably means he is a lardy.
- You can't rely on chemistry for that 'he may be handsome, but boy is he a jerk' gut feeling.
- If you do decide to meet, it is easier for someone to pull a no-show when they have never met you.
- With no human connection, trawling the internet for love can leave you feeling a bit empty and depressed.
- Without the social filter of meeting friends of friends, it is much more difficult to find someone 'like you'.

Follow these internet dating tips and see if you next love is just a click away:

- Go to it with low expectations. That way you won't be disappointed if all you meet are scoundrels and liars.
- Take time to present a good profile picture. After all, that is your calling card. You don't have to look super glam or up the sex appeal. A friendly smile, clean hair and a bit of makeup should do it.
- Don't act like a loved-up teenager. We all love that instant attention you get from internet dating – a smile here, a virtual wink there. You don't need to ping back a two-page email listing all your favourite films.
- Be mean to keep them keen: Internet dating is just the same as face-to-face flirting, so you can afford to let him chase you. Wait a day before you reply, after all, who wants people to think we are glued to our computer like a techy Norman no-mates?
- Be original: Have you noticed how everyone writes the same things. GSOH, love walking on the beach, log fires – they sound more like a Hallmark card than a prospective life partner. Try and stand out from the crowd.
- Don't be fooled. If it looks too good to be true, then it probably is.
- Beware if he puts 'looking for fun', on his profile. This does not mean a trip to the funfair or a comedy store. It means they are in it for a quick shag! If that is what you want, then fine. If not, leave well alone!

# FIRST DATE

So you have finally found someone and you want to date again. Whether it is the old-fashioned way, through friends or online, this one looks like it could be a runner. Now it's the giddy, scary time before that first date. After all, what is a date, if not two hours of romantic interrogation with the hope of sex and love at the end? Think of all that expectancy: will sparks fly? Will we find out we have friends in common and love the same things? Or will we both wish we were somewhere else?

## DATING RULES FOR THE MIDLIFE WOMAN

How can you ensure that your first encounter is the best it can be? Follow our step-by-step guide for first date success.

- Wear something that makes you feel fabulous. Don't buy a great dress that is too tight or scratchy or that makes you feel uncomfortable. You want to look your best but you also want to feel relaxed and be yourself. Try understated sexy with a touch of danger. A tight-fitting red dress is a sure way to get his heartrate soaring. If you opt for clingy, don't go too short and skimpy. Too much flesh on display over the age of 40 can look desperate.
- Don't have a radical image change just before the date. You may think that a new haircut or colour will give you a lift, but if it's a disaster you will spend the entire time checking yourself in the mirror or rearranging your funny fringe so much that your date might think he is dating a loony. Anyway, he likes the way you look or else he wouldn't be sitting opposite you.
- Leave plenty of time for pre-date preparation. Take a long bubble bath and moisturise afterwards. Apply your makeup with care. Overdo the hair products or the eye shadow and you could end up looking like a a desperate diva. Don't experiment with makeup at this stage. Go for your tried and tested formula.
- Don't wear a pair of shoes you find difficult to walk in. You will feel uncomfortable, look inelegant and may fall headlong into the waiter's arms before you even get to the table.
- Arrive at least 10 minutes late: this should ensure that your date is already waiting for you at the bar. If he isn't there – no one likes a man who is late – flirt with cute waiters and make him sweat.
- Be brave and break the ice. He may be even more nervous than you. Kiss him

hello on both cheeks, smile and compliment him.

- Avoid ordering complicated or messy food. You will either end up with a piece of spinach wedged in your molars, or you may put him off with strange slurping sounds, or choke on tiny fish bones. Why not try Moroccan mezze, Japanse or Spanish tapas, with a selection of different dishes on the table that you can share? It's a great ice-breaker and a short cut to bonding.
- Don't bring emotional baggage on the date. Your ex may be a sociopathic control freak, but going on about how he locked you in the hotel room on your honeymoon will only make you seem like a bitter old harpy. Show him your best flirty side.
- Be jokey. That doesn't mean you have to joshingly thump him on the arm or lean back in the chair and guffaw at his jokes. The art of first date chit-chat is to sprinkle your conversation with light, fun anecdotes. Say something amusing about what happened to you that day, or make a reference to a piece of news and make it funny.
- Create first date chemistry. Every now and then, disagree with what he is saying. It will make him slightly anxious, and as soon as you are nice to him again, he will warm to you.
- Disappear at some point – say you have to make a call to a friend/babysitter. At least five minutes will do. This will give him time to miss you, and when you come back, he will be more focused on you.
- Don't grill him about his relationship history. It will probably make him feel uncomfortable and you will look a bit of a psycho.
- Reveal a bit of leg or cleavage, but not both at the same time. It shows you are confident about your sexual power and playful.
- Don't get so drunk that you fall into the soup, trip up on the way to the restroom, or tell him you love him and start crying.
- Mix up the messages: 'Oh, you're very handsome, well-dressed and distinguished,' you say, smiling, then turn away and look into space. The more distant you are, the more this engages his interest. Make him work for your attention and he will think you are a prize worth having.
- Remember a date is a two way thing. You may be so nervous you find yourself babbling on about your children, job or mum. If you find your mouth running away with you, switch the conversation around to him and ask him what are his favourite films or places to go on holiday. Open ended questions are

a great way to keep the conversation going.
- If a date has been a success there will be a good night kiss and maybe an offer to go back to his place. Whatever you do, don't go home with him. Kiss him lingeringly and passionately on the lips as a promise of things to come, and say goodbye. Leave him wanting more and wait for the feverish good-night text that is sure to follow.

## DATE DUMPING

Of course, not all dates go as planned. Whilst your date may have sounded like George Clooney on the phone, how do you know if you will be sitting opposite a budding psychopath or a man with a bad case of halitosis?

It's time to dump your date if he:
- is rude to the wait staff.
- ogles other women at the restaurant or bar.
- is soooo boring, sticking needles in your eyes would be preferable to listening to any more of his stories.
- is so arrogant, he thinks you like him before you have even ordered your starter.
- spends the whole date checking emails on his Blackberry and tweeting.
- makes it obvious that he thinks you are no spring chicken and you are lucky to be with him.
- goes on and on about his ex.
- is ready to order the taxi after the first course.
- shows off about his job, car, cooking, house in the country …

# FIVE DEADLY DATING SINS

This dating malarkey is new for you and you may still be a bit rusty. Don't worry. Here are some of the gold-star dating no-nos everyone to avoid at the beginning of a relationship.

**Don't**

- Talk about your sexual past; dating is all about the here and now. Why dredge up a past husband or lover? It might sound fun slagging off the ex, but your new man is bound to think you're a bit of a bitch.
- Call him. It may be a few years since you were playing the dating game, but believe me the rules are still the same. Let him work a bit for your company. After all, men are hunters and like to think they are pursuing you – don't be easy prey.
- Give up your life for him. Just because you are in the 'best behaviour' dating phase, that does not mean you have to stop your salsa classes, girlie evenings or meeting your mum just to see him. Be unavailable. Don't always answer his calls. Create a bit of mystique at the beginning. It will set the tone and he will know that you are not a pushover
- Ask those girlie questions, such as: 'Does my bum looks big in this?', or whine, 'I can't go out, I'm soooo fat.' It is not endearing, it just appears needy. Wait until you are in a proper relationship to start digging out your insecurities. Ignore the red flags. If he is mean, cruel or plays mind games he is not a nice guy. If you make excuses for him, you will only find out later on.
- Ask where the relationship is going after only a few dates.

# MULTI-DATING

Dating is about getting to know each other. If you pin all your romantic hopes on one guy and he turns out to be a dud, you are bound to be comforting yourself with chocolate ice cream and wondering where it all went wrong. Keeping your options open. Dating several guys at the same time makes sense on many levels. Here are a few of the advantages:

- Remember what they say: success breeds success. All you need is two men giving you attention. Not only is it great for the ego, you start to feel attractive and sexy, and if you feel sexy, you will act in a more confident and sexy manner, which will attract more guys and so on until you are so sick of eating in wonderful restaurants, and your work desk is groaning under vases of flowers and boxes of chocolate, that you call it a day and marry one of them.

- If one of them starts to play games, doesn't call or is rude to you when you do speak, then having a whole list of back-up dates will put a stop to any screaming banshee behaviour. After all, who needs a withholding jerk when you have other nice men waiting in the wings.
- You will be so busy getting to know several guys at once that you won't have time for the 'where is this relationship going?' question we ask so often in our heads, and which, in a moment of insecurity or drunkenness may come hurtling out of our mouths – as he hurtles towards the door.

## THE TENDER TRAP

A few words on dating the younger man. The dating game has undergone a gender shake up in the past few years. What with Madonna, Susan Sarandon, Halle Berry and other celebrities stepping out with boys young enough to be their sons, more and more professional women are choosing to date down in midlife. Not surprising, really – after all, men have been doing it for ages. It's the old double standard in neon lights, with bells on! Wrinkly old septugenarians trying to cop off with or marrying 21 year-olds is perfectly natural, but when it comes to a 45 year-old woman dating a 30 year-old man, you can almost hear the cries of 'off with her head'.

The thing is, there are middle-aged women out there who are fed up with men their own age. What with their potbellies, wispy hair and midlife crises of their own, the male divorcee or old codger is not always a good catch.

Besides, maybe you are too busy climbing the career ladder for a full-on relationship with someone your own age. Or maybe you've had your heart broken too many times and you have decided it is time for a sweet young man who won't try to control you or put you down in front of your friends.

Besides, the old broad/young buck relationship has a lot going for it. It is a given that a lot of younger men find it very exciting and appealing to be with a woman who is confident, sassy and has her own flat in town.

**Pros of dating the younger man**

- They will always try hard to please. Many younger men are so chuffed they have bagged their very own Mrs Robinson that they will think nothing of rushing out at 4 a.m. for luxury ice cream, your favourite crisps and dips, or just to get you a bunch of flowers to say 'I love you'.

- They are relatively baggage-free. Without a divorce or kids in sight, the young man is free and full of fun. He is so sweet and hopeful that he will mop up your stories about the disco era and what it was like to actually go to a Rolling Stones concert.They are bendable, in more ways than one. The truth is, a younger man is more likely to go with the flow. Unlike some older men who bark orders at you like a sergeant major, he will love it if you take the lead and choose the film, restaurant or hotel.
- He is more affectionate. If you are licking your wounds after a nasty break-up, what better way to feel young and sexy again than a young man to lavish attention on you. Unjaded by a string of broken romances or a divorce under his belt, he is full of hope and sparkle. If he likes you, he is bound to text you many times a day, compliment you as if you are a Greek goddess, and leave little (inexpensive) gifts on your pillow.

# 9.
# CHANGE FOR THE BETTER
# HOW TO BE
# CONFIDENT AT MIDLIFE

# MIDLIFE MELTDOWN

It doesn't seem to matter if you are a happily married homebody, a midlife singleton or a busy career woman – as you cross over into your middle years, something starts to feel funny. You can't quite put your finger on it.

And then, bam!

You find yourself babbling excuses even when it is not your fault. You burst into tears if someone so much as looks at you the wrong way, and you can't step out of the door without phoning a friend and moaning and groaning about what you can't wear. 'My thighs have turned into cottage cheese, no one loves me anymore, I just want to slump onto the sofa and cry …' Aargh, pass the Kleenex.

So what's going on?

Of all the changes that women go through at midlife, this physical and mental slump can be the most scary. It's as if we are on a train, chugging along nicely and then – whoosh! It keeps getting derailed. One minute we are swanning through life with a spring in our step and the next we are gripped with a vague midlife ennui, our confidence eroding.

It is a lot harder for women today. Fifty years ago, come middle age, women were allowed to slip into a comfy chair with a cup of tea and a copy of *The Women's Weekly*. Nowadays, the race to stay young, in tune, toned up and slim until you're clapped out and in a nursing home, makes it harder to cope with the feelings we face at middle age. Sometimes it seems that society places all these expectations upon us and then calls us neurotic old harpies when we trip over ourselves trying desperately to live up to them.

Dare to bare a millimetre of cellulite and the world will gasp in horror; get a bit of liposuction and the world will brand you a vain, selfish woman who cares more about her appearance than world peace. See what I mean? We can't win either way.

So is it any wonder that our confidence and self-esteem are having a tough time working through all of it? What with the daily knocks, the competition to look like Demi Moore at 50, bake chocolate cake like Nigella Lawson and go for gold every time we step out of the door, don't you just feel that you want to escape to a desert island?

## TOP 10 MIDDLE WORRIES

- Help! I will soon turn into an old granny and dribble all day long.
- I have missed so many opportunities.
- The young intern with her swishy ponytail and Zeitgeisty know-how will soon be getting my job
- Every headache, twinge and niggle is bound to be a life-threatening disease.
- Unless I write everything down I will forget my own name.
- Forget wearing a bikini on the beach – it's more like a burkini.
- Everyone else is passing me by. Especially the friend with the book launch.
- I will never feel happy again.
- I will never be thought of as young and vital again.

## BIOLOGICAL BOMBS

As if life wasn't bad enough, at middle age our hormones suddenly start to go haywire: hot flushes, moods swings and night sweats. The perimenopause (a sort of pre-menopause that strikes us in our early to mid-40s) can have some unpleasant side effects. For some of us, they can be a mere inconvenience; for others it can feel like going through puberty all over again.

So how do you know if your hormones are playing havoc?

- You feel so tired all of a sudden, you just want to lie down in a darkened room and think of – well, nothing, actually.
- One minute you are laughing at your husband's joke, the next you are rushing into the next room crying your eyes out.
- You complain about having a headache every time the sex question is on the horizon.
- Your ankles look like balloons filled with water.
- Dare to laugh and you will pee at the same time.
- Every now and again you feel as if you are going to burn up from the inside like an erupting volcano.
- You get a roll of flab around your tummy, even if you are doing 5,000 sit-ups a day and running for hours on end.
- You start feeling like an angst-ridden teenager, but with wrinkles and grey hair.
- Your lady parts dry up like a parched river bed.

## FOODS TO AVOID

Levels of oestrogen start to drop in this pre-menopausal time, so if you are feeling a bit sluggish, it is best to cut down on refined or processed foods. These raise blood sugar levels and stimulate the release of the hormone insulin to mop up the excess sugar. This in turn negatively impacts the hormone balance. So that means avoiding anything containing white sugar, flour and rice. Also remember that drinking more than two alcoholic drinks a day will tax your liver, which can lead to hormones going haywire.

## SELF-ESTEEM WORKOUT

When we feel edgy and ill at ease, we can become difficult to talk to and even appear like a bit of a loony. This bad feeling about ourselves can undermine our relationships, which is a pity, because more often than not it is all in the mind. So in order to communicate better with those around you, you must first communicate with yourself. This means you need to have a good self-image.

Here's the top seven ways to be a sassy midlifer:

**The show-off list.** We could redecorate our bedroom, climb Mount Everest, and bake 100 cupcakes in a week, and women would still obsess about the one teensy spot on the end of their nose. The key to success is to turn off the negative chatter and start to boast about yourself. Write out a list of all the things that you are good at: you may speak another language, make beautiful drawings or simply be fun to be around. Writing them down acts as a reminder to yourself that you are at least good at some things! Then, when you're feeling a bit low, take the list out, read it, and add something new to it. If you're struggling to think of things to add to your list, then it's possible you're missing the obvious or being too harsh on yourself.

**Have some pluck.** Standing up for yourself is one of the quickest ways to feel good about yourself. Not only that, when others see you confronting the office bully or the grumpy bank clerk, it breeds confidence in others around you. Taking control of a situation will give you a newfound confidence, and any positive feedback you get from others will surely help with your levels of confidence, too.

**Ditch the doubt.** It might seem impossible to be a sassy midlifer if all you want to do is climb under the duvet and eat Ben & Jerry's ice cream. So stand in front of the mirror and try some positive affirmations. Repeating positive phrases such as 'I am successful' or I'm worth it,' can make a huge difference to a person's self-esteem. It might not seem like much but the more you repeat these upbeat mantras, the more likely you are to believe them.

**Step away from the comfort zone.** Okay, so we all like doing the same things and seeing the same people but getting stuck in the comfort rut will hold you back from being a sassy midlifer. Not only that, but how are you going to improve your life if you're stuck at home? Try a new thing every day: accept that invitation to the gallery opening or a party where you don't know anyone, or even just take a different route to work. Breaking with your usual routine also breaks the comfort cycle.

**Bounce back.** Any sassy midlifer develops an inner resilience – she knows setbacks and rejections are a part of life. Sure, it's stressful, but remember the only time you're not feeling some degree of stress is when you're six feet under. So what if the guy at the petrol station ignored you and flirted with the blonde in the sports car? Who cares? As soon as you let something get to you, you are on the road to a full-on crisis. Make a promise not to dwell on it and shift your focus onto something positive. Whether it is making sure you go to your yoga class or buy a new lipstick, if you change your thought, you are able to change your feeling.

**Always look on the bright side of life.** Instead of being dark and depressed about the way things really are, why not see a silver lining, even if you are having a horror of a day? Try turning things into positives and see how it works for you. Okay, so your friends and family may think you are a bit barking mad when you smile at them at 7 a.m. with waffles and freshly brewed coffee instead of the usual grunt and piece of burnt toast, but they will get used to the new you.

**Be kind.** If you want that warm fuzzy feeling deep inside all you have to do is give. Countless studies have proven that we are happiest when we are giving to other people. So instead of buying that new pair of leopard-skin leggings, why not give the money to charity instead? Feel better? Didn't think so. Maybe you should start small. Do something nice once a week, such as smiling at people, and you may find you feel better. And you can keep the jeans.

We can't always find a way to be brimming with inner confidence and self assurance. So if you are having a bad day, here are seven quick tips to give you a lift:

- **Stand tall and pull your shoulders back.** Often just little things like our posture can change how we feel. If you look like you mean business watch as people let you go to the front of the queue.
- **De-stress/re-stress.** Release tension from your body before a stressful situation. Gently roll your head and then stretch out your arms above you. Feel all that cortisol leaving your body. Breathe deeply and repeat.
- **Put on your all-time favourite happy music.** Upbeat sounds, especially if they are associated with good memories, will actually release feel-good hormones and give you a lift.
- **Left foot, right foot.** A brisk walk in the fresh air is a great tonic for when you are feeling a bit low. It is good for your heart and your brain, and every step is a step closer to a better bottom.
- **Thump a cushion.** Scream and shout. Okay, so this one may not be advisable to do in public unless you want to end up in the dock. But if you are stressed, releasing these pent-up feelings can give you a real feel-good surge and it's not a bad workout either.
- **Imagine.** If thumping the cushion hasn't worked, try this. Take a moment to close your eyes and imagine a place of safety and calm. It could be an image of you walking on a beautiful beach or snuggled up in bed watching a DVD with George Clooney. Let these positive feelings flood over you until you feel more relaxed – only don't start murmuring his name if your partner is in the vicinity.
- **It's not about you.** It pays to understand that people's actions, even when hurtful, rarely have anything to do with you. When your friend is short with you or sounds a bit flat it does not mean that she has decided to drop you from her friend list, it is probably because she has just had an argument with her partner, children, or any other manner of thing. Seeing everything as a slight to our personality can trigger negative stressful feelings. People are people; there's never a need to link their behaviour and your happiness. Knowing this gives you the freedom to feel confident.

## ARE YOU SUFFERING FROM STRESS-OREXIA?

Today's middle-aged woman is smart, sassy and sorted. We have broken the glass ceiling, we earn our own money and yoga is a way of life, so why are so many of us struggling to get out of bed in the morning?

Come middle age, so many women find themselves up against a phalanx of tedious chores, emails to answer, shopping to do, loved ones to nurture, bodies to slim, the drycleaning, the broken tumble dryer – you know the script. So how do you know if your hectic schedule is giving you more than a headache?

You're running on empty if:

- Your day is punctuated by coffee runs, and you are only happy when you feel the caffeine rush. You snack on sugary treats to keep your energy levels up.
- You feel tired all the time, even after a good night's sleep.
- You are suffering from constant brain fog and sleep walking through the day.
- The thought of sleep is more appealing than the thought of sex.
- The only relationship you are having is with your alarm clock.
- The last time you leapt out of bed was back in your 20s.
- You're always breathless – and not in a good way.
- You are having a digital relationship with your loved ones.
- You are snippy and jumpy, and you don't even know why.
- You suffer queue rage... you don't have time to wait.
- Too much excitement and you have to lie in a darkened room for at least a day afterwards.
- You feel constantly guilty about the avalanche of chores left undone.

## HOW NOT TO FEEL SHATTERED

So how do we break free from the cycle of constant busy-ness and noise?

**Pick up a pint.** It may sound like something your mother would say, but a glass of warm milk at bedtime can really help you to get off to sleep. It contains calcium and tryptophan, which help you get a good night's rest. If the body is tired but your mind is whirring through the day's events, read before you nod off. Concentrating on something other than yourself can help calm down your negative chatter.

**Cut down on the caffeine.** You don't have to ditch the double espresso in the morning; after all, we all need our daily pep-me-ups, and we'll do anything that helps us smile through the morning meeting or school drop-off. But be careful – caffeine is a powerful stimulant, so if you're already stressed and your adrenaline is flowing, it can tip you over into the 'jangly zone'. As a rule, drinking more than three or four coffee-shop coffees a day probably isn't a good idea.

**Learn to breathe.** When you feel stress taking over, concentrate on breathing slowly and deeply. When stressed, you tend to breathe shallowly, using movements that involve only the upper part of your rib cage. Your shoulders tend to rise up towards your ears, with little expansion of your abdomen. To improve your breathing technique, breathe in through your nose and out through your mouth, and try to empty your lungs completely before taking the next breath.

**Take a break.** When it all becomes a bit too much, stop and take time out. Find a chair and sit comfortably or lie down on the bed, if you are at home. Turn off all the lights, close your eyes and breathe calmly and slowly. Consciously relax the muscles in your face, hands, arms, shoulders and legs, and feel your body as it releases the tension. Clear the mind and just breathe deeply until you feel ready to face the world again.

**Turn off the harrumph button.** We all do it. You are walking along, cursing the rain, the noisy traffic that is disturbing your phone call. And who are those kids making all that noise? Whoa! You are giving yourself a whole load of stress. The next time you catch yourself getting irritated by life, find something to be positive about. Notice the colour of the trees or the way that man smiled at you. When you notice the good things, you start to relax and your mood lifts.

**Put yourself on a digi-free diet.** Most of us have far too much techno-noise in our life and this can cause overload stress. Why not turn off Twitter, sign off from Facebook, and stop your inbox for a while? Okay, so some emails are important, but the amount of junk emails, and group email jokes that bored friends inundate us with, can become too much. Unsubscribe to any newsletters, politely tell your friends not to send you any more jokes or those irritating email chain letters, and read a good book instead.

# HOW TO SPARKLE AT A PARTY

Can I get away with saying that I have just sprained my ankles and sorry, I am not going to make your party tonight? Or that I will have to postpone the dinner with my work buddies, as the water pipes have burst and I am standing in a puddle up to my knees?

According to psychologists, approximately six out of 10 middle-aged women are thought to suffer such a crisis of social confidence that they will invent any excuse to stay at home and avoid meeting new people.

Sound like you? Probably not. But haven't we all been gripped with the 'OMG no one will like me, I have fat ankles, I look old' fear?

If you think you may be having a bit of a party panic, here are a few tips to get you over the hurdle:

*Make a diva entrance.* Before you walk into a party, stop and take a few deep breaths. Make sure your posture is good and that you have a smile on your face. Look around as if it's your party; this will give you an air of confidence and relaxed control. As you walk, keep your hands by your side. Don't rush across the room like a baboon on speed – you want to appear to glide. If in doubt, check out some old Hollywood movies. The lead actress always makes a statement entrance.

*Welcome with body language.* Before you even open your mouth, you are communicating how you feel. You may look hot to trot, but if you are feeling anxious, you will be sending out 'I'm panicking' signals. If you want to sparkle at a party, you need to send out open, friendly body signals that say, 'Come here, I'm fun to talk to.' Sitting up straight with a relaxed posture shows that you are having a good time and are interested in people. If you are standing, uncross your arms and keep your palms facing upwards. If you send out friendly signals then you will get friendly messages back.

*The power of small talk.* There is simply no point slinking into a corner and munching on crudités like a scared little mouse. Making small talk is so important as it starts the conversational ball rolling, which can lead to greater things.

You don't have to rush over to the first sympathetic person and plant a big wet one on his or her cheek. But once you see someone you want to chat to, position yourself close enough to get a good look and wander over casually. Begin with an easy 'open' question. They're the type you can't answer yes or no to, and start with words such as how, where, why and are. So, 'How was your journey?' or 'How do you know the host?' are good first lines, as they are easy to answer but also easy to elaborate on if they want to.

**Smile.** The most magnetic people are immediately identifiable by the fact that they greet everyone with a warm smile. You don't need to have a naturally cheerful manner, it is about making an effort. No matter how you are feeling, if you can manage to produce a warm smile, it is the first step to developing natural magnetism. Research shows that if you look at someone and then smile, it instantly charms them.

**Be a charmer.** Charm is seduction without sex and a potent party technique. The method is simple. All you need to do is deflect attention from yourself onto the other person. Simply try to understand their spirit, match their mood, and make them feel great. Ask questions about their lives and pepper the conversation with supportive statements such as 'uh-huh,' 'yes, I see', and 'how interesting'. It will soften them up and they will drop their defences.

## LEARN TO SAY 'NO' AND STILL BE POPULAR

Do you have difficulty saying 'no'? Are you always trying to be nice to others, even at the expense of your own wellbeing? Well, you're not alone. So many women suffer from 'too hard to please' syndrome, which basically just means you're a decent person and you don't want to hurt the other person's feelings. The problem is, when we take on too much we end up resenting the whole damn lot of them.

For example: You agree to make the cakes for the summer fete again because it felt rude to say 'no'. You pick up your partner's new shirt and the shopping because you are a kind soul at heart. You simultaneously take a work call and cook a healthy meal with baked quinoa and fresh vegetables for the family because you want them to be healthy. Meanwhile, you couldn't make it to the hairdresser, so your hair looks like a frizzy hedge and you are so exhausted you crawl into bed and collapse with your makeup on.

Maybe now is the time to learn the 'N' word. To learn to say 'no', you first have to find out what it is that is stopping you in the first place:

Here are the five main reasons that a lot of women find it hard to say no:

- You are a nice person and you always want to help others, even if it eats away at your own time.
- You are afraid of offending. Saying 'no' seems so rude.
- You don't want them to reject you.

- You are scared of confrontation.
- You don't want to burn bridges.

**What to do:**

- Set boundaries. That doesn't mean you have to drape yourself in barbed wire, but understand what is acceptable and what is not.
- Don't lie just so that you don't hurt the other person's feelings. Being truthful is always the best course of action.
- Buy some time. For most of us the word 'yes' flies out of our mouth faster than a Concorde. So just say, 'Can I get back to you on that?' Don't let people push you around.
- Filter through reason. When someone asks you to pick up little Johnny (on the other side of town) because she is sooo busy, ask yourself if you have time. The key to saying 'no', and feeling good about it, is a question of whether you should put your needs ahead of others. Sometimes it is right to put others' needs first – we all want to help out our friends and loved ones from time to time – but we need to balance that with looking after our own interests as well.
- If you find it too hard to utter those two little letters, practice in front of the mirror or start with situations where it doesn't matter so much.
- Learn some easy ways to say no without offending anyone. *Start with a sweetener:* 'It's great to hear from you.' *Then go in for the kill:* 'I can't commit to this as I have already committed to someone (or something) else,' or 'Now is not a good time, could you call me another day?' *Turn it into a question:* 'Does it have to be tonight?' *Give them some alternatives:* 'Maybe we could find someone else to make the nativity costumes.' *Finish by changing the subject:* 'Have you seen those wonderful shoes they have on sale in the city?' Congratulations, now go and have a glass of wine. You deserve it!

# Quiz

How confident are you? Find out by taking our fascinating little quiz.

**1 When you look at yourself in the mirror in the morning, what is the first thing you think?**
a) Who is that gorgeous young thing?
b) Mmm, could do with putting makeup on.
c) Eww, throw a paper bag over it, please.

**2 You are going to a karaoke party and everyone has to choose a song. Which one would you do?**
a) 'Feeling hot hot hot…' That will get the party going and give you the opportunity to show off your dancing.
b) A nervous rendition of something simple.
c) Are you joking? I don't do karaoke.

**3 Over the past few months, have you generally thought positive things about yourself?**
a) I always have positive thoughts about myself and what I can do.
b) I try to think good things, but I can often run myself down.
c) I have constant negative chatter going on in my head, which makes me feel bad.

**4 You have been invited to a party and turn up overdressed. Do you:**
a) Not care and think you look good anyway.
b) Worry about it a bit, have a drink, and then forget about it.
c) Go home and change.

**5 You have been asked to give a speech at a wedding. Do you:**
a) Start preparing it straight away. You love talking in front of an audience.
b) Feel a bit nervous, but do it anyway.
c) You are terrified of public speaking and invent an excuse to get out of it.

**6 You are starting a new job. Do you:**
a) Feel excited. You love new challenges.
b) A bit nervous. You know you can do it, but new things throw you a bit.
c) You have your head down the loo being sick!

**7 A friend is raving about a movie that you thought was rubbish. Do you:**
a) Engage in an interesting conversation about the film.
b) Wait to see what other people say before you give your opinion.
c) Keep quiet, no cares what you think anyway.

**Mostly A's:**
You have a high self-esteem, and don't mind who knows it. Never one to shrink back, you are the first to start boogying on the dance floor, the first to introduce yourself, the first to get the party going. And when you do feel out of your depth in a social situation, you fake it – after all, what have you got to lose? Just be careful you don't put on a brave face all the time. Sometimes it pays to show our vulnerabilities.

**Mostly B's:**
You fluctuate from feeling confident with bouts of low self-esteem to feeling pretty good about yourself. Learn to love yourself and others will love you. You lack drive and have forgotten how to take risks. Don't worry so much about taking on a challenge. Even if it is singing a song at karaoke, small risks are where it all begins.

**Mostly C's:**
Oh dear, you live with constant negative chatter in your head and a fear of standing apart from the crowd. You need to stop rubbishing yourself. If you rubbish yourself, you will rubbish everything around you, which in turn will make you feel more negative. Adjust the negative voice in your head and focus on positive things. Make yourself do some of those embarrassing things. You may find they are not as bad as they seem, and once you start, it gets easier.

# 10.

# HITTING THE ROCK CONCERTS

## HOW TO REINVENT YOURSELF AND HAVE FUN

# IT'S NOW OR NEVER

Something kicks in when you reach your middle years. Call it a wake-up call, a sudden realisation that life is not a dress rehearsal, or simply that it is time to make the most of what we've got. One thing is definite: after you've been plodding along nicely for decades, tending to the family, putting other people's needs first, or simply living life, an inner voice starts to make itself heard.

'It's my turn!' it bellows as it comes roaring out of the closet, as if it has taken on a life of its own.

Indeed, after a period of thumb-twiddling, crying rivers and a glimpse into a future of bifocals and bedpans, women in their 40s start to get into fifth gear. They take salsa classes, find a new job, ride a Harley round Mexico, or even get an age-inappropriate tattoo.

After all, what is the point of a midlife crisis, if not a last attempt to have fun and take on new challenges before the slow slide into decrepitude and doddering?

And now, for the first time, women can take control of midlife on their own terms, not their husband's, their children's, or society's for that matter. 'It's now or never', they are saying, as they strap on their skydiving outfit and jump headlong into the unknown.

The trouble is, after decades of putting other people's needs above our own, we may have forgotten how to jump. Here are the top excuses we make so that we can stay in our comfort zone

**I'll make changes when:**
- My back gets better.
- I get enough money.
- The children leave home.
- The hubby is not so tired.
- I'm not so knackered all the time.
- My mother/father/aunt gets better.
- I get slimmer/fitter/happier.

The thing is, it's important to shake things up a bit as you get older. Try new things, break new boundaries and reinvent yourself. Go line dancing in America, take that evening class you always wanted to.

You're middle-aged, for God's sake, not in your dotage!

And it doesn't matter what you do, whether it is learning how to sing, staying out all night or learning how to be a pole dancer, feeling good in midlife is about finding out what makes you tick. Here are some ideas.

## Dirty dancing

If you're more at home in support tights than stockings and suspenders, and more used to exercising your brain than your seductive powers, try these two dance class and get fit and foxy at the same time.

- *The tango:* They call it vertical sex, and for good reason. The tango – that twisty sexy dance with those dark, Latin, undertones – is vigour enhancing, stress busting and enough to get the middlie juices going. Think of all that eye gazing, back arching and head tossing. If you manage not to trip over or get a cricked neck, the simple act of putting your arms round someone and letting them move you can make you feel alive and is as sexy as hell. Not to mention it is a wonderful workout that is bound to leave you feeling energised and ready to paint the town red!

- *Be a hurly burly girl:* If you're more cuddly puppy than rampant sex kitten, maybe a quick lesson in high kicks and doing funny things with feather boas could be the perfect way to unleash your inner minx. We spend so much time swathed in jeans, trainers, and doing tedious chores that sometimes our inner erotica can get lost. Attending a burlesque class and learning how to tease, peel off gloves and walk like a pin-up, can do wonders for the middlie self-esteem. Finding out that your body can give you pleasure and that, with a bit of effort, it will do things you never thought possible, is an empowering feeling, and a workout in itself.

## Join a band

If you have been harbouring secret yearnings to be the next Carly Simon or Suzi Quatro, then why not join a band? The greatest thing about starting a band in your 40s is that you don't have to worry about record deals or becoming famous and you get to unleash all those pent-up rock star dreams. Whether you are twanging a guitar or belting out *Jumping Jack Flash*, what better way to feel young again than jamming through your crisis.

## Go bungee jumping

Whoosh! That feeling of jumping into thin air is an exhilarating thing. Having spent decades stuck in offices, at home or paying the gas man, taking a leap of faith into the unknown can be a life-affirming event. Whether it is about getting over a fear of heights or simply a way to relieve yourself of pent-up stress, bungee jumping is another notch on your midlife achievement belt.

## Be a graver (granny-raver)

Relive your memories of all-night raves and feel the freedom of the music festival. Stomping through fields up to your knees in mud, drinking beer out of plastic cups and watching the sun come up over the hills, if you haven't lost your appetite for partying and nature, then get your middle-aged kicks and become a graver.

Okay, so you may want to rethink the tent – comfort over cost and that kind of thing. Plus the inexorable march of time means that loud music and raging hangovers are not what they used to be.

Back then, you:

- Couldn't afford a tent so you slept under the stars and prayed it didn't rain.
- Pulled an all-nighter and carried on partying through the weekend.
- Drank beer and vodka shots and still felt fine.
- Went for a curry afterwards and got up for work on Monday morning.
- Went to any rave that was going on.
- Wore bikini tops and cut-off shorts.

Now, you:

- Buy a top-notch tent, good quality pillow, insulated sleeping bag and apple-scented shower gel.
- Pull a muscle after five hours of non-stop raving.
- Drink beer and book into a luxury hotel afterwards.
- Have a massage and spend the next three days in bed.
- Carefully choose a venue with a hotel, bar and good restaurant nearby just in case.
- Wear sensible shoes and wellies.

## Midlife camping

You fall asleep dreaming of communing with nature, the smell of fresh coffee brewing on the camp stove and sizzling sausages ready to be eaten.

Then you wake up. Whatever childhood memories you may have are of pitching tents in the bucolic countryside and watching the sheep gambolling across the fields as the sun goes down. In reality you:

- Wake up all through the night to step outside for a pee and because of the bloody noise. Your mattress deflates, it's cold, you've never been so uncomfortable in your life …
- Queue for the showers, restrooms and the cafeteria – in short, anything you do at a campsite involves lots of standing around.
- Bring lots of fleeces because it gets very cold at night in a tent.
- Instead of feeling calm and collected, all you feel are bugs and creepy-crawly things moving across your face as you sleep.
- Eat stodgy campsite food, or bring your own.
- Throw in the towel and decamp to the nearest B & B or hotel.
- Bring a saucepan to catch the rainwater when the tent starts to leak.
- Never know why or how, but everything always seems to get wet, even the sleeping bag.

## THINGS TO DO BEFORE YOU'RE 50

A lot of us go through life with a sense of growing regret about the places we have not visited, the books we have not read and the things we have never managed to do.

Here are the top things every woman should do before the mists of time descend:

- Throw a proper party. Not one of those polite middle-aged dinner parties where everyone sits around and talks about mortgages and school fees. Get a DJ and play all your favourite tunes. Then invite everyone you like and dance till dawn.
- Go skinny dipping at midnight in Italy.
- Read a great philosophical work. There is nothing to make you feel more satisfied than absorbing the thoughts of a great mind.
- Make love in the lift, in the shower, on the kitchen floor or in a park.
- Attend a really major rock concert.
- Learn to speak a foreign language and then go practise it.
- Learn to love yourself naked.
- Go deep-sea diving.
- Swim with dolphins.
- Work in a soup kitchen for a few days and realise how fortunate you are.
- Book a romantic weekend away – drink champagne and eat caviar.

- Go camping somewhere hot.
- Spend a day in bed reading, watching trashy Hollywood movies and eating chocolate and ice cream.
- Stand on top of Niagara Falls and feel the spray on your face.
- Learn to be brave.
- Go on a luxury cruise.
- Learn how to cook like a professional.
- Go trekking up the final section of the Inca Trail to Machu Picchu.
- Write that book you always said you had in you.
- Go white-water rafting.

## UNLEASH YOUR INNER FUNSTER

Somewhere along the line between childbirth and painting the house magnolia, women have forgotten how to have fun. Not surprisingly, having spent our lives climbing career ladders, potty training or bringing up a tribe of unruly teenagers, we seem to have put our own enjoyment on the back burner. There always seems so much to do: make the dinner, load the dishwasher, get a leg wax, lose weight, give up sugar, deal with the divorce. Aargh, it's never-ending.

## STUMBLING BLOCKS TO MIDLIFE FUN

You:

- Wake up and think 'What must I do today?'
- Micromanage your children's life.
- Go to dinner parties that end at 11 p.m. Everyone wants to be in bed before midnight.
- Look forward to your favourite DVD box set.
- Rush home to pay the babysitter.
- Plan everything and put it in the diary. Spontaneity is off the agenda. Even going for a coffee after school drop off requires the planning of an SAS mission.

Hang on a minute!

We may have lost the battle with inner-thigh flab and grey hair, but that doesn't mean we have to give up. We can still have pleasure, can't we? Good grief, men enjoy themselves all the time. Whether it is the pub, the late night curry with their mates or a round of golf on a Sunday, men have always managed to carve out their slices of 'me' time. Well, now it's our turn. To unleash your inner funster:

- Give yourself permission to have fun.
- Turn off the 'To Do' button.
- Step away from the cooker and get a takeaway.
- Stop thinking you have to look after everyone.
- Learn how to play.
- Stop being so hard on yourself.
- Reward yourself. You deserve it!
- Give the kids to the relatives and take a day off to wander around the city
- Whether it is a couple of hours a week or blocking off an entire weekend, set aside fun time.
- Tell the family you're scheduling regular 'me' time, and stick to it.
- Practise saying 'no' to all those chores.
- Book a spa weekend and sleep till noon.
- Make new friends and go to new places.
- Hire a cleaner to do the housework, even if it's just once a fortnight.

## GIRLS JUST GOTTA HAVE FUN

For women, when it comes to fun, not everyone is patting us on the back. There's no mistaking the signs. You're at a party or dinner and you've had a bit too much to drink. You are laughing a bit too loudly and throwing your arms in the air as you tell a funny story. Whether it is the teenage daughter rolling her eyes at her embarrassing mum or the husband grinding his teeth as you balance a spoon on your nose, the message is the same: 40-something women should be sedate, demure and enjoy nothing more challenging than an evening at their book club.

Bah humbug! It's time to get out of the comfort zone. While a part of us may want to take the easy route and slump on the sofa with a good book and a glass of wine, we all have another side that wants to knock back the tequilas and dance on tables. Sometimes we simply need to let our hair down and leave our responsibilities at home.

## FIVE RULES OF BEING A 40-SOMETHING PARTY GIRL

So you want to paint the town red and dance on the tables? Here are some tips to get you started:

- **Do what you please.** The 40-something party girl is answerable to nobody, neither children nor husband. She can get drunk, behave badly and the only thing she has to contend with is a hangover in the morning.
- **Learn how to give as good as you get.** Okay, so you are not going to be the youngest, prettiest girl in the room, but at midlife our success has less to do with a perfect figure and silky décolleté and more to do with attitude. A 40-something is more likely to floor a man at 50 paces with well-placed witticisms.
- **Mix up your plans.** Put a big red line through the weekend plans and go out clubbing with the girls. Lie in late and leave all the laundry and other tedious tasks till Monday.
- **Summon up the energy.** The likelihood of fun coming to you is slim, so don't leave it to chance. Even if you feel that you're too tired or busy, what's the big deal? We all have those too-weary-to-lift-our-feet-off-the-floor moments. So take a shower, put on your favourite music, and have a martini. You'll feel party fit in no time.
- **Don't be fashion road kill.** Dress up, wear a mini by all means, but squeezing into bandage dresses if you are not twiglet thin will only make you look like a cougar – which is fine, if that is what you are going for.

## SO ARE YOU A 40-SOMETHING PARTY GIRL?

Say yes if you:

- Dance to 70s funk and soul.
- Are a free spirit in touch with your basic impulses.
- Go commando in a sparkly dress and do a handstand.
- Stay out till all hours and leave the husband a note.
- Love a bit of danger – and go after it.
- Make bawdy jokes and knock back the tequila slammers.

- Have stopped thinking it's a man's world.

40-something party girl is:

- most likely to say, 'Pass the champagne'.
- unlikely to say, 'I go to yoga at 6 a.m. every morning'
- most likely to wear negligees and Jimmy Choo mules that flick off as she lies on the sofa.
- most unlikely to wear slacks and Birkenstocks.
- most likely to be found at posh weekend parties in the country, causing trouble, or at bars where she can misbehave without being banned.

## Midlife party girls

Tracey Emin

Courtney Love

Madonna

Kate Moss

## Mature party girls

Dolly Parton

Vivienne Westwood

Marianne Faithfull

Joan Collins

Liza Minnelli

Joan Rivers

## Vintage party girls and their mottos:

- Marilyn Monroe: 'If I had observed all the rules, I'd never have gotten anywhere.'
- Mae West: 'Sometimes it seems to me I've known so many men that the FBI ought to come to me first to compare fingerprints.'
- Tallulah Bankhead: 'I'm as pure as the driven slush.'
- Dolly Parton: 'I modelled my looks on the town tramp.'

The thing is, having fun keeps you feeling and looking young. It's good for your mood – it gets rid of stress and anxiety. It's good for your health – it unleashes all those feel-good hormones. And there is nothing like the heady exhilaration of dancing naked in the rain, skinny dipping in the sea, or simply watching our favourite movies to make you feel GTBA (good to be alive).

Sometimes that GTBA feeling can get buried under layers of work, responsibilities and all the other sensible stuff that can make us lose touch with our inner desires.

## DO YOU FEEL GTBA?

Say yes if you:

- Dance in the kitchen naked.
- Are more likely to see the funny side of things.
- Walk barefoot in the grass.
- Book a holiday on the spur of the moment.
- Dance in the rain.
- Swim in a river.

Say no if you:

- spend your evenings watching television.
- have an attack of 'OMG I'll be tired' angst if you are not in bed by 10 p.m.
- drink alone.
- love it when your friends are down and come to you with their problems.
- refuse to smile because it gives you wrinkles.
- stay in bed till midday in a darkened room.

# THE CALL OF THE WILD

Do you sometimes feel when you get up in the morning that there must be more to life than this? The cooking, the cleaning, sitting in traffic jams, and the slow slide into flab and fondue.

Do you sometimes feel irritable just because?

Do you always want better/more?

Sometimes, even if our lives tick all the boxes – cute husband, nice job or house, almost sane kids, a pleasant enough life on the outside – there comes a point when we start to get restless, flip out … you can't put your finger on it, but then the penny drops:

You need a change. You're bored. You're bored of listening to the same songs on your iPod, going to the same place for holidays. What you need is an adventure!

Kayaking up the entire length of the Amazon, climbing Kilimanjaro, trekking through the Gobi desert? Are you kidding? A strenuous workout at the gym is probably the toughest thing most of us have ever done. Not because we can't, not because we probably wouldn't want to once we had made the effort, but because we are petrified of stepping outside the box.

Climbing mountains, swimming long distances, sailing on the ocean wave, and other dangerous pursuits call on parts of us that we have long since neglected in the safety of modern life. Our whole lives are consumed by children, work and the daily routine to get through it all, so that it can seem a bit drastic to up and go round the world on the back of a camel.

Will you? Won't you?

Here are some of the things we tell ourselves that stop us taking that leap:

- Act your age!
- You're past your prime.
- You're over the hill.
- You'll get sick.
- Your family can't do without you.
- You can't swim.
- Your life is pleasant enough as it is.
- You always go away to that nice place near the beach, why change now?

Don't put your future on hold: it is time to wake up and hear the call of the wild!

Here are some things to kick start your sense of adventure:

- You don't know the meaning of the word blisters until you have trekked for hours in rough terrain.
- Taking on a tough physical challenge makes you feel as if you are really alive!
- You walk like a cowboy who has just stepped off a horse because your legs are so tired.
- You feel drunk on excitement and exhausted at the same time.
- Hanging off a rock face in 50-degree heat puts all your problems into perspective.
- You are pushing your limits and finding out there is so much more to you.
- Mascara and lip gloss are the last things on your mind.
- You dream of a comfy bed and central heating.

- You lose 10 pounds and get a fabulous sun tan.
- Nothing matters. You are living in the now.
- You can commune with nature and creepy-crawlies.
- You will take time out from your usual routines.

## THE MIDLIFE CRISIS TRIP

Who said adventurous travel was for teenagers and students on their gap year? The midlife adventurer, complete with her backpack and sturdy walking shoes, is becoming a common sight in hostels, on mountains and around the world. And it makes sense – you are willing to try climbing Kilimanjaro but unlikely to get into a car with drunken strangers. That, and you are unlikely to be phoning your parents for emergency cash or to get you out of an overcrowded foreign gaol.

## THINGS TO CONSIDER WHEN PLANNING YOUR MIDLIFE CRISIS TRIP

**Find out what you like.** Do you want to see the wildlife, take a physical challenge, a road trip, or see the sights? By knowing what you want, you will avoid finding yourself stuck up the side of the mountain thinking, 'I should have picked the Hawaii trip.'

**Check before you book.** Don't just pick up the first brochure advertising a safari in Kenya, and go 'Yaaay! I've always wanted to see the lions!' Safaris are great but are not the relaxed holiday you may think. You will need to be prepared for dawn starts, eating at midnight and bumping along in a rickety Range Rover at five in the morning.

**Pack the right clothes.** This one sounds simple, but so many people get it wrong. If you are trekking in hot weather then you need to go to specialist outlets and pick the right materials to stop overheating and/or getting so many blisters you have to be escorted back home!

**Check the weather.** If you are the type to lounge in the heat, then booking a trip to Cape Town in the winter will be disappointing. And Antarctica, Canada or Seattle – forget it.

**Be original.** Think beyond the brochure. Pick places off the beaten track, otherwise you might find yourself sharing your crisis trip with a million other cranky midlifers.

**Train.** If you are taking on a physical challenge, make sure you are in the right physical condition. There is no point getting halfway through a 70-mile bike ride and finding yourself on a stretcher. You can always ask at your local gym and put yourself through the paces in the comfort and warmth of your local fitness studio first.

Of course, after you come back from your six months helping children in Africa or a road trip across America, you may find yourself at odds with your 21st century cosseted life.

On your return:
- You are in shock for a week.
- You have forgotten what those funny buttons you have to press to cross the road are for.
- Your family have forgotten who you are and have sublet your room.
- You prefer to sleep on the floor.
- You eat insects from the garden.
- You have lost the knack of good conversation.
- You are sick of working at the computer company and you change jobs.
- You change husbands.
- You go and live in another country.

# REINVENTING YOURSELF

For some women, the trip of a lifetime is enough to sort out that restless midlife angst. For others they have a gut feeling that they need to make bigger changes in their life. And its funny because at exactly the age when many men start feeling jaded and tired with their same old life, and slob out in dirty tracksuit bottoms drinking beer, women start to feel there is no time to waste. They want to turn their lives around and do something completely different before time runs out. They've poured their energy into their children, home, husband or community and now they want to find the person they truly are. It's as if one day you wake up and realise you've been wearing the wrong clothes and they don't fit any more.

## GOING BACK TO SCHOOL

Do you ever wish you were doing something a bit cleverer than the school drop-off or mowing the lawn? You kid yourself you're not bored and you convince yourself that your synapses are like rusty wires that won't work any more. Going back to university may seem scary to begin with and you may think you are an oddity sitting in a room full of teenagers, but becoming a student a second time around will expand your horizons and give you a great sense of achievement. Alternatively, universities and colleges provide day and evening classes that lead to a certificate.

## CHANGING CAREERS

By your mid-40s you may find yourself stuck in a job that you know deep down isn't really you. It was never really you, but back then you had to make ends meet, pay the school fees or just live. You always knew you had something else inside and had been treading water all these years. Then one morning you wake up and think, 'Today I am handing in my notice, because you know what? I don't ever want to talk to Mary in Personnel, file any more accounts, or sit at that goddamn desk anymore.'

We are women who have reached a certain age. We've done a lot, seen a lot and now we are sick of doing the same commute, smiling at the same faces and sharing the same gossip at the water cooler. And we are prepared to risk our job security to find out what lurks within.

So how do you know when you are having a temporary case of the humdrum work-place blues, or if you really are in a full on work crisis?

You know you're ready to change paths when:
- Your performance goes off track.
- You start to wonder why you are there and consider shooting the boss.
- You want to throw paper darts at your colleagues instead of getting down to work.
- You never meant to stay in computing, banking or sales, it was always meant to be a temporary job.
- There are more cons than pros.

**What to do**

- Find a job you don't enjoy. Life is too short to spend your days stuffing envelopes
- If you want a second chance career, then focus on how to make it happen.
- Think about your childhood dreams.
- Come home and tell your partner you've resigned. You don't need his blessing, but his support would be nice.
- Take courses in art, learn a language or go for long walks.
- Enrol at university and do an MA.
- Take over the spare room and make your own art.
- Take a creative writing course and write that novel or children's book. Make the family ready-meals and write in your spare time.

Whether you decide to become an ageing party girl, take a round-the-world trip or study for a PhD in micro-economics, every change we make is an opportunity to grow and enrich our lives.

Looking forward to the second half of our lives can be scary, but exciting as well. Whether you want to take the midlife bull by the horns or sit back and have another cupcake, you are already equipped with everything you need to make the life that you want to live and be the person you want to be.

So keep on trucking! And good luck!

## Acknowledgments

I would like to thank everyone at New Holland, especially Fiona Schultz, Diane Ward and Alan Whiticker for all their support and enthusiasm. Thanks to my wonderful agent, Fiona Spencer Thomas, a beacon of calm and serenity. And thanks to all the friends who have chatted late into the night about life, love and being middle-aged. Thanks girls!

First published in 2013 by
New Holland Publishers
London • Sydney • Cape Town • Auckland
www.newhollandpublishers.com • www.newholland.com.au

Garfield House 86–88 Edgware Road London W2 2EA United Kingdom
1/66 Gibbes Street Chatswood NSW 2067 Australia
Wembley Square First Floor Solan Road Gardens Cape Town 8001 South Africa
218 Lake Road Northcote Auckland New Zealand

A catalogue record of this book is available at the British Library and at the National Library of Australia

ISBN: 9781742573281

10 9 8 7 6 5 4 3 2 1

Publisher: Alan Whiticker
Project editor: Kate Sherington
Designer: Kimberley Pearce
Production director: Olga Dementiev
Printer: Toppan Leefung Printing Limited

Follow New Holland Publishers on
Facebook: www.facebook.com/NewHollandPublishers